Alan Jacobs has made a lifelong study of mysticism. He is a regularly published author and poet and an accomplished anthologist. He compiled the highly-acclaimed anthology, *Poetry for the Spirit* and assembled and edited *The Essential Gnostic Gospels*, *Native American Wisdom*, *Tales from Rumi*, and the beautiful poetic translations of *The Gnostic Gospels* and *The Upanishads*.

By the Same Author:

Poetry for the Spirit
The Essential Gnostic Gospels
Native American Wisdom
Tales from Rumi
The Gnostic Gospels
The Upanishads

PEACE
of
MIND

*Words of Wisdom to
Comfort & Inspire*

Alan Jacobs

WATKINS PUBLISHING
LONDON

This edition published in the UK 2010 by
Watkins Publishing, Sixth Floor, Castle House,
75–76 Wells Street, London W1T 3QH

Text Copyright © Alan Jacobs 2010

1 3 5 7 9 10 8 6 4 2

Designed by Jerry Goldie Graphic Design
and typeset by Dorchester Typesetting

Printed and bound in China

British Library Cataloguing-in-Publication data available

ISBN: 978-1-906787-66-0

www.watkinspublishing.co.uk

Contents

Acknowledgements

The Author and Publisher wish to thank all those contributors and copyright holders too numerous to mention who have given their permission for an extract to appear. If, however, there are any omissions the author and publisher will be pleased to correct the matter in any future editions.

To Michael Mann for suggesting this compilation.

To the helpful staff and great resources of the British Library without whom this book would not have been possible.

FOREWORD

Perhaps the one quality, more than any other, that we human beings earnestly desire is Peace of Mind.

I have consequently compiled this major Anthology, packed full of wise and beautiful selections of Prose and Poetry, to assist everyone who delves into its pages to find the necessary help and inspiration to achieve this blessed state.

There is no doubt that we live in difficult times. There are very many fine men and women, either feeling apprehensive about the future or perhaps regretting the past. Into each life, sooner or later, some unwanted drops of rain must fall. Nevertheless I am certain that in this book, the reader will find some choice quotation or poem, which will provide the strength and capacity to overcome any sorrow. I trust it will help them joyfully return to an optimistic state of mind, poised to forge a happy and contented future.

In this book the many gifted authors who have contributed have all taken a highly positive view of life, and see our challenging world as a glorious adventure, a wonderful opportunity to heroically surmount all life's difficulties come what may!

Alan Jacobs
London, July 2009

Dedicated to my grandchildren
Jacob, Hannah, Sarah, Jack and Louis

– *Achievement* –

Action

Let us, then, be up and doing,
    With a heart for any fate;
Still achieving, still pursuing,
    Learn to labour and to wait.

Henry Wadsworth Longfellow

Achievement

That man is a success who has lived well, laughed often and loved much; who has gained the respect of intelligent men and the love of children; who has filled his niche and accomplished his task; who leaves the world better than he found it, whether by an improved poppy, a perfect poem or a rescued soul; who never lacked appreciation of earth's beauty or failed to express it; who looked for the best in others and gave the best he had.

Robert Louis Stevenson

1

Endeavour

If one advances confidently in the direction of his dreams, and endeavors to live the life which he has imagined, he will meet with a success unexpected in common hours.

Henry David Thoreau

– *Beauty* –

I never saw an ugly thing in my life: for let the form of an object be what it may – light, shade, and perspective will always make it beautiful.

John Constable

On the Beach at Night

On the beach at night, Stands a child with her father, Watching the east, the autumn sky. Up through the darkness, While ravening clouds, the burial clouds, in black masses spreading, Lower sullen and fast athwart and down the sky, Amid a transparent clear belt of ether yet left in the east, Ascends large and calm the lord-star Jupiter, And nigh at hand, only a very little above, Swim the delicate sisters the Pleiades. From the beach the child holding the hand of her father, Those burial clouds that lower victorious soon to devour all, Watching, silently weeps. Weep not, child, Weep not, my darling, With these kisses let me remove your tears, The ravening clouds shall not long be victorious, They shall not long possess the sky, they devour the stars only in apparition, Jupiter shall emerge, be patient, watch again another night, the Pleiades shall emerge, They are immortal, all those stars both silvery and golden shall shine out again, The great stars and the little ones shall shine out again, they endure, The vast immortal suns and the long-enduring pensive moons shall again shine. Then dearest child mournest thou only for Jupiter? Considerest thou alone the burial of the stars? Something there is, (With my lips soothing thee, adding I whisper, I give thee the first suggestion, the problem and indirection,) Something there is more immortal even than the stars, (Many the burials, many the days and nights, passing away,) Something that shall endure longer even than lustrous Jupiter Longer than sun or any revolving satellite, Or the radiant sisters the Pleiades.

Walt Whitman

Think of all the beauty still left around you
and be happy.

Anne Frank

Beauty and Beauty

When Beauty and Beauty meet
All naked, fair to fair,
The earth is crying-sweet,
And scattering-bright the air,
Eddying, dizzying, closing round,
With soft and drunken laughter;
Veiling all that may befall
After – after –

Where Beauty and Beauty met,
Earth's still a-tremble there,
And winds are scented yet,
And memory-soft the air,
Bosoming, folding glints of light,
And shreds of shadowy laughter;
Not the tears that fill the years
After – after –

Rupert Brooke

The ability to see beauty is the beginning of our moral
sensibility. What we believe is beautiful we will not
wantonly destroy.

Reverend Sean Parker Dennison

The Breadth and Beauty
of The Spacious Night

The breadth and beauty of the spacious night
Brimmed with white moon light, Swept by winds
    that blew,
The flying sea spray up to where we two,
Sat all alone, made one in Love's delight –
The sanctity of sunsets palely bright;
Autumnal woods, seen 'neath meek skies of blue,
Old cities that God's silent peace stole through,
These of our love were very sound and site.

The strain of labour; the bewildering din
Of thundering wheels; the bells' discordant chime;
The sacredness of art; the spell of rhyme,
These, too, with our dear love were woven in,
That so, when parted, all things might recall
The sacred love that had its part in all.

Phillip Bourke Marston

Develop interest in life as you see it; in people, things,
literature, music – the world is so rich, simply throbbing
with rich treasures, beautiful souls and interesting people.
Forget yourself.

Henry Miller

Tranquil Thoughts

Golden rays dancing on dragonflies' wings,
  Iridescent colours sparkling like jewels,
A babbling brook, ripples touched with gold,
  Many-splendoured hues my eyes behold.

Lying, longing for you to be nigh,
  Golden leaves above me
Softly, silently stirring by the gentle breeze
  Which breathes a fairy sigh.

Golden head bows over buttercups yellow,
  Petals touched at their tips
With sunshine from the Elfin's broch.
  Thoughts cascading like millions of
    shooting stars in the heavens.
Those gentle hands, I feel their touch.

C. R. Bruce

People often say that 'beauty is in the eye of the beholder', and I say that the most liberating thing about beauty is realizing that you are the beholder. This empowers us to find beauty in places where others have not dared to look, including inside ourselves.

Salma Hayek

And beauty is a form of genius – is higher, indeed, than genius, as it needs no explanation. It is of the great facts of the world, like sunlight, or spring-time, or the reflection in dark waters of that silver shell we call the moon. It cannot be questioned. It has its divine right of sovereignty. It makes princes of those who have it.

Oscar Wilde,
The Picture of Dorian Gray (ch. 2)

The Pageant of Summer

Besides the singing and calling, there is a peculiar sound which is only heard in summer. Waiting quietly to discover what birds are about, I become aware of a sound in the very air. It is not the midsummer hum which will soon be heard over the heated hay in the valley and over the cooler hills alike. It is not enough to be called a hum, and does but just tremble at the extreme edge of hearing. If the branches wave and rustle they overbear it; the buzz of a passing bee is so much louder it overcomes all of it that is in the whole field. I cannot define it, except by calling the hours of winter to mind – they are silent; you hear a branch crack or creak as it rubs another in the wood, you hear the hoarfrost crunch on the grass beneath your feet, but the air is without sound in itself. The sound of summer is everywhere – in the passing breeze, in the hedge, in the broad-branching trees, in the grass as it swings; all the myriad particles that together make the summer are in motion. The sap moves in the trees, the pollen is pushed out from grass and flower, and yet again these acres and acres of leaves and square miles of grass blades – for they would cover acres and square miles if reckoned edge to edge – are drawing their strength from the atmosphere. Exceedingly minute as these vibrations must be, their numbers perhaps may give them a volume almost reaching in the aggregate to the power of the ear. Besides the quivering leaf, the winging grass, the fluttering bird's wing, and the thousand oval membranes which innumerable insects whirl about, a faint resonance seems to come from the very earth itself. The fervour of the sunbeams descending in a tidal flood rings on the strung harp of earth. It is this exquisite undertone, heard and yet unheard, which brings the mind into sweet accordance with the wonderful instrument of nature.

Richard Jefferies *The Life of the Fields*

Landscape

A still sheet of water in silver evening light
under a faint blue sky, six white swans sailing slowly
over the dim reflections and the gleaming ripples;
a group of dark-bough'd graceful leafless elms and beeches
spreading their slender arms across the pure pale sky;
gentle music of birds and far off cries of children,
and a cool soft air blowing and great peace in my heart.

Vivian de Sola Pinto

The words that enlighten the soul
are more precious than jewels.

Hazrat Inayat Khan

Intercourse With Waves and Sky

The sun comes bursting from my heart.
I see it lift above the waves.
The veils of the clouds stand still
and round them spread great, sweeping
pools of light, as though
a river speeds and swirls
about these acres of the sky.

Each cell of me is whirled
into this dance, where all of me
is colours, which the hands
of breeze are lapping and consuming,
as I try to find the words to speak
this ordinary moment,
where I live and die.

And what bewilders me
and batters at my ignorance, is why
I am not glad enough to be,
at every moment of my time,
in such amazing company,

for it has never been away,
and even as I grieve for what I miss,
this moment of my loss
is full with colour and with life,
that fills me and ignites me with its kiss.

Kevan Myers

God's World

O world, I cannot hold thee close enough!
   Thy winds, thy wide gray skies!
   Thy mists that roll and rise!
Thy woods, this autumn day, that ache and sag
And all but cry with color! The gaunt crag
To crush! To lift the lean of that black bluff!
World, world, I cannot get thee close enough!

Long have I known a glory in it all,
   But never knew I this:
   Here such a passion is
As stretcheth me apart. Lord, I do fear
Thou'st made the world too beautiful this year;
My soul is all but out of me, – let fall
No burning leaf; prithee, let no bird call.

Edna St. Vincent Millay

– *Brilliance* –

Chasing Brilliance

I thought of something quite brilliant
not too long ago,
and where that thought escaped to
God will only know.
I'm pretty sure it had to do
with humanity.
The results and outcomes of which
would last an eternity.
Or maybe it involved
the matter of conservation.
The enlightenment it would bring
would induce worlds of conversation.
Or it must have delved into
the goal of exploration.
The thought einsteinic in nature
of thorough innovation.
I thought of something quite brilliant
not too long ago,
But it's destiny was not to be remembered
or else I would still truly know.

Kaz Kawasaki

Winter in Regents Park

Over an iced and sparkling lake,
colonies of white gulls settle.
Skeletal trees feather distant palladian palaces.
In burning bush, a sleeping drake
warms his beak in his wing,
with webbed feet wide on frosty ground.

Here, where the sword
pierces my heart, are points
of dazzling fire that dance
on dark water flowing.

The rhythm of angels never repeats,
as a galaxy forms on the deep.

The rose is alive in January;
her deep, red kisses are frost enfurled.
To hear the falling water all around,
is a wider sense than seeing;
for they throw water and the milk of mares
     over deity.
Waters from the fountains here
froth a tangle of fish's tails.

Jane Adams

It is precisely because we resist the darkness in ourselves that we miss the depths of the loveliness, beauty, brilliance, creativity, and joy that lie at our core.

Thomas Moore (*Dark Nights of the Soul*)

Love's Brilliance

In the light of dawn
I feel your skin on mine

I turn to face you
And see your smile

As brilliant as the morning sun
Flowing through the curtains

Your eyes shine like gems
As your gaze meets mine

A smile spreads across my face
As I recall love from evening last

The smile resides in my heart
When you are near to me.

Lillian Jamison

At present I absolutely want to paint a starry sky. It often seems to me that night is still more richly coloured than the day; having hues of the most intense violets, blues and greens. If only you pay attention to it you will see that certain stars are lemon-yellow, others pink or a green, blue and forget-me-not brilliance. And without my expatiating on this theme it is obvious that putting little white dots on the blue-black is not enough to paint a starry sky.

Vincent Van Gogh

– *Calm* –

Calling us Home

Deep within us all there is an amazing inner sanctuary of the soul, a holy place, a Divine Centre, a speaking Voice, to which we may continuously return. Eternity is at our hearts, pressing upon our time-torn lives, warming us with intimations of an astounding destiny, calling us home unto Itself.

Thomas R. Kelly

Solitude

All alone – alone,
Calm, as on a kingly throne,
Take thy place in the crowded land,
Self-centred in free self-command.
Let thy manhood leave behind
The narrow ways of the lesser mind:
What to thee are its little cares,
The feeble love or the spite it bears?

Let the noisy crowd go by:
In thy lonely watch on high,
Far from the chattering tongues of men,
Sitting above their call or ken,
Free from links of manner and form
Thou shalt learn of the wingéd storm –
God shall speak to thee out of the sky.

Edward Rowland Sill

The Inner Life

It is those who have a deep and real inner life who are
best able to deal with the irritating details of outer life.

Evelyn Underhill

Calm

Store up reservoirs of calm and content and draw on them
at later moments when the source isn't there, but the need
is very great.

Rupert Brooke

Stillness

Only a bell and a bird break the stillness …
It seems that the two talk with the setting sun.
Golden coloured silence, the afternoon is made
   of crystals.
A roving purity sways the cool trees
and beyond all that,
a transparent river dreams that trampling over pearls
it breaks loose
and flows into infinity.

Juan Ramon Jimenez

Fear

Nothing in life is to be feared,
   it is only to be understood.

Mme. Curie

A Celtic Benediction

DEEP PEACE
of the Running Water to you.
DEEP PEACE
of the Flowing Air to you.
DEEP PEACE
of the Quiet Earth to you.
DEEP PEACE
of the Shining Stars to you.
DEEP PEACE
of the Son of Peace to you.

Anon

Self Control

He that would govern others,
first should be the master of himself.

Philip Massinger

True Silence

True silence is the rest of the mind; it is to the spirit what
sleep is to the body, nourishment and refreshment.

William Penn

When the mind is at peace,
the world too is at peace.
Nothing real, nothing absent.
Not holding on to reality,
not getting stuck in the void,
you are neither holy nor wise, just
an ordinary fellow who has completed his work.

Layman P'ang

Liquid Transactions

Stillness creates
pictures on the water.
See how the shapes and colours
put up their feet, and stretch,
in liquid ease,
along this chair.

A diving bird
will re-arrange
the universe:
exchanging every
masterpiece, for leaves
of silver, scattered
on the waves.

And eyes that gaze
upon this transformation
do not know
if they are simply
glasses into which
this liquid pours
with all its art.

Or could it be clear water
where the eyes see only
colours, which are painted
by their heart?

Kevan Myers

Self Restraint

Remember that there is always a limit to self-indulgence,
but none to self-restraint.

M. K. Gandhi

Dive Deep

If we go down into ourselves we find that we possess
exactly what we desire.

Simone Weil

The Peace of Wild Things

When despair for the world grows in me
and I wake in the night at the least sound
in fear of what my life and my children's lives may be,
I go and lie down where the wood drake
rests in his beauty on the water, and the great heron
    feeds.
I come into the peace of wild things
who do not tax their lives with forethought
of grief. I come into the presence of still water.
And I feel above me the day-blind stars
waiting with their light. For a time
I rest in the grace of the world, and am free.

Wendell Berry

Horse Chestnut

Roots and the stand of
heavy breasted summer trees
are silence in my being
    before and after
boys come with sticks
to batter the surface of this moment
for conkers, shedding leaves.

Jane Adams

– *Confidence* –

You Have Wings

You were born with potential.

You were born with goodness and trust.

You were born with ideals and dreams.

You were born with greatness.

You were born with wings.

You are not meant for crawling, so don't.

You have wings.

Learn to use them and fly!

Rumi

Myself

I celebrate myself, and sing myself,

And what I assume you shall assume,

For every atom belonging to me as good belongs to you.

I loaf and invite my soul,

I lean and loaf at my ease observing a spear of
summer grass.

Walt Whitman

I Am

I *am* – the power of self-knowledge
I *think* – the power to investigate
I *know* – the power to master facts
I *feel* – the power to appreciate, to value, to love
I *wonder* – the spirit of reverence, curiosity, worship
I *see* – the power of insight, imagination, vision
I *believe* – the power of adventurous faith
I *can* – the power to act and the skill to accomplish
I *ought* – the power of conscience, the moral imperative
I *will* – will power, loyalty to duty, consecration
I *serve* – the power to be useful, devotion to a cause.

George Walter Fiske

– *Courage* –

I've Looked

I've looked over, and I've seen the promised land.
I'm not worried about anything. I'm not fearing any man.

Martin Luther King Jnr.

Profile in Courage

To be courageous requires no exceptional qualifications, no magic formula, no special combination of time, place, and circumstance. It is an opportunity that sooner or later is presented to us all. Politics merely furnish one arena which imposes special tests of courage. In whatever arena of life one may meet the challenge of courage, whatever may be the sacrifices he faces if he follows his conscience – the loss of his friends, his fortune, his contentment, even the easteem of his fellow men – each man must decide for himself the course he will follow. The stories of past courage can define that ingredient – they can teach, they can offer hope, they can provide inspiration. But they cannot supply courage itself. For this each man must look into his own soul.

John F. Kennedy

Courage

Nothing but courage can guide life.

Vauvenargues

Keep Your Fears

Keep your fears to yourself,
but share your courage with others.

Robert Louis Stevenson

What is more mortifying than to feel that you've missed
the plum for want of courage to shake the tree?

Logan Pearsall Smith

Courage is rightly esteemed the first of human qualities
because it is the quality which guarantees all others.

Winston S. Churchill

Whatever you do, you need courage. Whatever course you
decide upon, there is always someone to tell you that you
are wrong. There are always difficulties arising, which tempt
you to believe that your critics are right. To map out a
course of action and follow it to the end, requires some of
the same courage which a soldier needs.

Ralph Waldo Emerson

Courage is the price that life exacts for granting peace. The
soul that knows it not, knows no release from little things,
knows not the livid loneliness of fear; nor mountain heights
where bitter joy can hear the sound of wings.

Amelia Earhart

We learn courageous action by going forward whenever fear urges us back. A little boy was asked how he learned to skate. 'Oh, by getting up every time I fell down,' he answered.

David Seabury

The great virtue in life is real courage, that knows how to face facts and live beyond them.

D. H. Lawrence

Courage is not merely one of the virtues but the form of every virtue at the testing point, which means at the point of highest reality.

C. S. Lewis

… the big courageous acts of life are those one never hears of and only suspects from having been through like experience. It takes real courage to do battle in the unspectacular task. We always listen for the applause of our co-workers. He is courageous who plods on, unlettered and unknown … In the last analysis it is this courage, developing between man and his limitations, that brings success.

Alice Foote MacDougall

If

If you can keep your head when all about you
Are losing theirs and blaming it on you,
If you can trust yourself when all men doubt you
But make allowance for their doubting too,
If you can wait and not be tired by waiting,
Or being lied about, don't deal in lies,
Or being hated, don't give way to hating,
And yet don't look too good, nor talk too wise:
If you can dream – and not make dreams your master,
If you can think – and not make thoughts your aim;
If you can meet with Triumph and Disaster
And treat those two impostors just the same;
If you can bear to hear the truth you've spoken
Twisted by knaves to make a trap for fools,
Or watch the things you gave your life to, broken,
And stoop and build 'em up with worn-out tools:
If you can make one heap of all your winnings
And risk it all on one turn of pitch-and-toss,
And lose, and start again at your beginnings
And never breathe a word about your loss;
If you can force your heart and nerve and sinew
To serve your turn long after they are gone,
And so hold on when there is nothing in you
Except the Will which says to them: 'Hold on!'
If you can talk with crowds and keep your virtue,

Or walk with kings – nor lose the common touch,
If neither foes nor loving friends can hurt you;
If all men count with you, but none too much,
If you can fill the unforgiving minute
With sixty seconds' worth of distance run,
Yours is the Earth and everything that's in it,
And – which is more – you'll be a Man, my son!

Rudyard Kipling

Many women miss their greatest chance of happiness
through a want of courage in the decisive moments
of their lives.

Winifred Gordon

Courage is required not only in a person's occasional crucial
decision for his own freedom, but in the little hour-to-hour
decisions which place the bricks in the structure of his
building of himself into a person who acts with freedom and
responsibility.

Rollo May

Courage is sustained ... by calling up anew
the vision of the goal.

A. G. Sertillanges

Nil Desperandum!

Courage brother! Do not falter,
    Dry your tears and cease from sighing;
Though clouds look black, they soon may alter,
    And the sun will send them flying.

'Out of evil oft cometh good,'
    Is a maxim to my liking;
The blacksmith well the iron beateth,
    But 'tis better for his striking.

Work today and give up grieving,
    Know that joy is born of sorrow;
And though today is rainy weather,
    Hap 'twill brighter be tomorrow.

Gambling doth not make our labour
    The least bit more a pleasant task;
'Tis joyful heart that lightens trouble,
    Contentment brings to those who ask.
First the childhood, then the manhood;
    First the task and then the story;
'Tis after nightfall comes the dawning,
    First the shade and then the glory.

Abdullah Quilliam

It requires moral courage to grieve;
it requires religious courage to rejoice.

Søren Kierkegaard

We must assume our existence as *broadly* as we in any way can; everything, even the unheard-of, must be possible in it. That is at bottom the only courage that is demanded of us: to have courage for the most extraordinary, the most singular and the most unexplicable that we may encounter.

Rainer Maria Rilke *Letters to a Young Poet*

When it comes to the pinch, human beings are heroic.

George Orwell

Courage which goes against military expediency is stupidity, or, if it is insisted upon by a commander, irresponsibility.

Field Marshal Erwin Rommel

Great things are done more through courage
than through wisdom.

German Proverb

Brian Gibbon

Brian Gibbon, a fourteen-year-old schoolboy, lay in bed one morning, thinking it was time to get up. Suddenly there was the thundering noise of an aircraft close overhead. A deafening crash and the room seemed to fall about him as it filled with dust and smoke.

Brian leapt out of bed. He reached for his young nephew, Tommy, who clutched at him in terror. The room was on fire. Brian pulled a rug from the floor, rolled Tommy in it, and pushed him on to the bed.

'Stay there!' he ordered. 'I'll see if we can get out of the window!'

He pushed open the window. Below, in the front garden, neighbours had gathered. They stretched out a blanket when they saw him and yelled:'Jump, lad, jump!'

To their horror, Brian turned back into the blazing room. Half-blinded by smoke, he felt on the bed for Tommy. He wasn't there. Brian found him on the floor, still bundled up in the rug, too terrified to move. Brian lifted him up and carried him through the flames and smoke to the window.

Below, the neighbours waited, still holding out the blanket. Brian lifted his bundle on to the window sill, pushed it over and watched it fall into the outstretched blanket.

Tommy was safe.

By now, Brian's pyjamas were on fire, burning his back and chest. But he managed to clamber on to the window-sill and jump. He too was caught in the outstretched blanket and rolled in it, then he was lifted gently into the ambulance that had just arrived and taken to hospital.

No one thought Brian would live, he was so badly burned. But the doctors and nurses were as determined to save his life as he had been to save Tommy's. They nursed him day and night until he was out of danger.

It needs courage to fight pain and not give in to it, but Brian had plenty of courage. It had saved Tommy's life, now it helped Brian to recover. One thing worried him. His mother did not come to see him. He asked for her but was told she could not come. It was only when he was considered strong enough to hear the truth, Brian was told all that had happened on that morning of September 2nd, 1958.

At 7.00 a.m., a Viking aircraft had taken off from Heathrow Airport, which was just a mile or two from Brian's home in Southall. The plane left the runway without any trouble but it had not gone far when it got into difficulties and crashed down on to the roofs of two houses, one of which was Brian's home.

The aircraft smashed into the houses, setting them on fire with the petrol that poured from its fuel tanks. Three of the aircraft's crew were killed instantly, so were Brian's mother and the children next door. His father was injured and so were Tommy's parents, but their injuries were not severe and they had already recovered.

Only one person from the two houses had not been injured, and that was Tommy.

As soon as Brian was well enough to have visitors, Tommy went to see him in hospital. The little boy was too young to understand all that Brian had done for him. All the same, it must have been a great moment for them both. Brian had saved the little boy's life by his courage and cool, unselfish action.

Brian did recover from his burns after many months in hospital. During that time he often needed as much courage as he had shown when he went through the flames to save Tommy.

Seven months later, in April 1959, he was awarded the George Medal by Her Majesty the Queen.

A woman who is courageous has to conceal the fact if she wishes conventional men to like her. The man who is courageous in any matter except physical danger is also thought ill of.

Bertrand Russell

– *Creativity* –

The Lord of the Dance

The whole creation is dancing; the whole universe – galaxies, nebulae, stars and their satellites – is engaged in the Great Dance. They turn, and come together, and draw apart, and come together again. And so it has ever been, and so it shall ever be through all eternity.

Creation makes it own music. There is no created being that does not sing, and the music of everything that is joins together to make the great Harmony and Rhythm of the Dance. Everything that exists treads the same measure, each according to its own rhythm, and every individual rhythm is related to, and is an integral part of, the Rhythm of the Dance. These rhythms are reflected in the life-cycle of beings, and there is no part of creation which does not have its own life-cycle, whether they be creatures of a day, like some insects, or plants, or trees, or men, the rocks and the rivers, and earth itself, the stars and indeed the whole Universe as it is known to man … The whole Universe is a dance measure, and the measure of the Dance itself determines the shapes and patterns of creation. The Measure, and the Rhythm of the Measure are one and the same, and everything that exists expresses the central theme of the Dance, each in its own way. This central theme is Love.

Anthony Duncan

When Earth's Last Picture Is Painted

When Earth's last picture is painted and the
   tubes are twisted and dried,

When the oldest colours have faded, and the
   youngest critic has died,

We shall rest, and, faith, we shall need it – lie
   down for an æon or two,

Till the Master of All Good Workmen shall put
   us to work anew.

And those that were good shall be happy: they
   shall sit in a golden chair;

They shall splash at a ten-league canvas with
   brushes of comets' hair.

They shall find real saints to draw from –
   Magdalene, Peter, and Paul;

They shall work for an age at a sitting and never
   be tired at all!

And only The Master shall praise us, and only
   The Master shall blame;

And no one shall work for money, and no one
   shall work for fame,

But each for the joy of the working, and each, in
   his separate star,

Shall draw the Thing as he sees It for the God of
   Things as They are!

Rudyard Kipling

Lack of visualization makes it impossible to be enlightened, for enlightenment is to fill the mind with pictures of light that we see all round us, thus making our minds as like the universe as we possibly can. This beautifies the mind and ends our alienation from reality. And this is only the start, visualization is the foundation on which we build the nine dimensions of intelligence that Einstein used, moreover, we can go far farther, for it leads us towards the ultimate human intelligence.

Every one of the additional dimensions adds to the wonder and beauty of the enlightened mind: imagination, intuition, creativity, vision, the subconscious, super-conscious, and full use of the creative hemisphere of the brain, which give us humans promise of some day being able to think like Newton and Einstein and the astrophysicists of the cosmos. Or we can aspire to writing the transcendental poetry of Rumi that gives the highest joys of the mind; there are no outside joys greater than those in our own minds.

Tahasa Falconar

Poem of our Homeland

Painter, you use a million colours
But what good are they if your heart is grey?
Your palette runs in rivers of colour
But are your life's pages black on white?
Take up your palette of meditation.

Paint the mind's sky with the blues of pity
And its fields with the greens of love.
 Fill your whole life with colours.
 Make your body a house of pictures.
 Let the prisms of the flowers,
 Spin the light into long films
 That run in the mind's playhouse.
Let your eyes be stained windows
To dye the texture of your days
So the hours of your life will pass by
Like a kaleidoscope's glittering parade.
 Watch the photons spread their bright wings,
 These micro-butterflies of the spectrum.
 And fly like fireflies flashing
 Through forests of burning light
Coloured photons enter the eyes' lenses
And escape into the vastness of the tundra.
And like ice crystals on the windows
They freeze and become the light flowers
That bloom on the endless snow fields
Like beacons blazing in the mind's galleries.

Tahasa Falconar

– Crisis –

This too will Pass

I was taught these words by my grandmother as a phrase that is to be used at all times in your life.

When things are spectacularly dreadful; when things are absolutely appalling; when everything is superb and wonderful and marvellous and happy – say these four words to yourself.

They will give you a sense of perspective and help you also to make the most of what is good and be stoical about what is bad.

This too will pass

Claire Rayner
The motto above the Count of Monte Cristo's castle

He that climbs the tall tree has won right to the fruit.
He that leaps the wide gulf should prevail in his suit.

Sir Walter Scott

My dear thing, it all comes back, as everything always does, simply to personal pluck. It's only a question, no matter when or where, of having enough.

Henry James

The beauty of the soul shines out when a man bears with composure one heavy mischance after another, not because he does not feel them, but because he is a man of high and heroic temper.

Aristotle

No coward soul is mine; No trembler in the world's
  storm-troubled sphere:
I see Heaven's glories shine,
And faith shines equal, arming me from fear.

Emily Brontë

Pick yourself up,
Dust yourself down,
And start all over again.

Frank Sinatra

If the Creator had a purpose in equipping us with a neck,
  He surely meant us to stick it out.

Arthur Koestler

That which does not kill me makes me stronger.

Friedrich Nietzsche

Everlasting Arms

Disasters, trials and troubles come all down Life's
    stony way

for loss and griefs and agonies are with us every day

and hearts are breaking all around

the world's a sad old place

You'll see some tragic story told in every passing face .... .

Our loved ones pass from out our sight the sunshine
    disappears

and we are left to face the bleakness of the empty years.

Where is the key that will unlock the golden gates of
    peace?

Where is the balm that heals our wounds and brings
    the heart release

from all the fruitless questing, and the passion and
    the pain

the infinite desire for one who will not come again? ...

There is one consolation given to the human race

there is one hope of peace

there is one quiet and secret place

Safe from Life's blows, its treacheries, its terrors and
    alarms ...

For underneath, we're told there are the
    Everlasting Arms.

Patience Strong

Remember that there is nothing stable in human affairs;
therefore avoid undue elation in prosperity, or undue
depression in adversity.

Socrates

Present suffering is not enjoyable, but life would be worth
little without it. The difference between iron and steel is
fire, but steel is worth all it costs. Iron ore may think itself
senselessly tortured in the furnace, but when the watch-
spring looks back, it knows better.

Maltbie Davenport Babcock

Perhaps statistics would show that most calamities
never happen.

George Abbott

Never go out to meet trouble.
If you will just sit still, nine times out of ten
someone will intercept it before it reaches you.

Calvin Coolidge

Misfortunes come on wings and depart on foot.

H. G. Bohn

Don't be a catastrophizer. When forecasting events, there is often a temptation to fixate on worst-case scenarios in the name of being prepared. However, this approach usually causes unnecessary angst – things are rarely as bad as we expect. In such situations, take sensible precautions, but make it a rule not to preoccupy yourself with fears of imagined future disasters.

Decouple your worries. When worries are lumped together they can seem so overwhelming that your entire life becomes one big insurmountable problem. Instead, try separating out your worries so that you can deal with each one individually. When you do this, each worry seems smaller and as a result easier to understand and ultimately deal with.

Retune your memories. Look back over any memories from the past that continue to cause you emotional pain. Examine your story of what happened. Try to separate the factual events from your interpretation. Is there a more positive way that you can interpret these events?

Mike George

In trouble to be troubled
Is to have your trouble doubled.

Daniel Defoe

Most of our misfortunes are more supportable than the
comments of our friends upon them.

C. C. Colton

Oh, a trouble's a ton, or a trouble's an ounce,
Or a trouble is what you make it,
And it isn't the fact that you're hurt that counts,
But only how did you take it?

Edmund Vance Cooke

What is a romantic? One who, when life is too banal or too
lazy to manufacture tragedy for him, creates it artificially,
thus getting himself into the hot water he himself
has boiled.

Clifton Fadiman

You have no idea how big the other fellow's troubles are.

B. C. Forbes,

The biggest problem in the world
Could have been solved when it was small.

Witter Bynner

– *Diligence* –

Keep on Learning

The mind is like a muscle. It grows strong with use. Do something every day to discipline your mind. Undertake a hard task. Find a way out of some difficulty. Keep records and do some writing regularly. Learn to estimate and criticize your own work. Allow time for daily reading. Read newspapers with discrimination and give more time to books. Use free public libraries. Form a library of your own. Spend at least as much for books as you do for movies. Include biography, history, poetry, science, and current affairs. Avoid the trivial and the vulgar. What goes into the mind comes out in the life. Select what goes into your mind as carefully as you do the food that nourishes your body. Your mind is the master key to the good life. The first mark of a student is an appreciation of the worth, dignity, power, and usefulness of his own mind.

Anon

Always Finish

If a task is once begun
Never leave it till it's done.
Be the labor great or small,
Do it well or not at all.

Anon

The Art of Concentration

A good player keeps his eye on the ball. That is the secret of
skilled workmanship. The hand follows the eye. Where one
looks he strikes. The mind is like that. Many problems
which seem difficult become simple when one keeps his
mind upon them, holding it there, or bringing it back over
and over again until the solution appears. Each time you
assert mastery over your mind it becomes easier to control.
You can train for occasions of great mental performance
even as the athlete trains for the Olympic Games. Just as
the long distance runner begins slowly and each day goes
further, you can train your mind until it is able to perform
sustained mental tasks with joy and vigor. Keep your mind
where you want it to be. Thus you will develop that most
precious possession, a disciplined mind – ready, accurate,
courageous, and trustworthy.

Anon

Develop Your Skills

The part that one can play among his fellows is determined
by skills of mind and hand and body, by the mastery that
one has over brain, eye, nerve, and muscle. Can you
maintain a conversation in a pleasing voice? Can you walk
with ease and poise? Can you tell a story? Can you sing? Play
an instrument? Can you dance? Can you drive a car safely?
Can you set a table? Dress a baby? Make a budget? Can you
make a flower bed? Saw a board? Drive a nail? Make repairs

about the home? Can you typewrite? Take shorthand? Give directions or take them? Make a satisfactory application for work? Preside over a meeting? Make a speech? These are all skills. They can be developed by sustained practice. Skill gives joy and a sense of worth. Choose one skill after another and work at each until you attain excellence and establish habit.

Anon

Value of Work

The happy people are those who are producing something; the bored people are those who are consuming much and producing nothing … Boredom, then, is a certain sign that we are allowing our faculties to rust in idleness. When people are bored, they generally look about for a new pleasure, or take a holiday. There is no greater mistake: what they want is some hard piece of work, some productive drudgery. Doctors are fond of sending their fashionable patients to take a rest cure. In nine cases out of ten a work cure would do them far more good.

Dean Inge

Work

There are few purer sources of happiness than the consciousness of having actually made or produced something good of its kind. Whether the product be useful, or beautiful, it is the same. If it was worth doing, and if we have done it, or rather, are doing it, joy results. But the joy is greater in proportion to the spiritual value of the thing produced. A great work of art, or a great scientific discovery, gives greater joy to its maker than a work of merely technical or mechanical skill.

Dean Inge

The Spirit of the Worker

Life is indeed darkness save when there is urge,
And all urge is blind save when there is
knowledge,
And all knowledge is vain save when there
is work,
And all work is empty save when there is love;
And when you work with love you bind
yourself to yourself, and to one another,
and to God.
And what is it to work with love?
It is to weave the cloth with threads
drawn from your heart, even as if your beloved
were to wear that cloth.

It is to build a house with affection, even as if
   your beloved were to dwell in that house.

It is to sow seeds with tenderness and reap the
   harvest with joy, even as if your beloved
   were to eat the fruit.

It is to charge all things you fashion with a
   breath of your own spirit.

From _The Prophet_ by Kahlil Gibran

– _Dreams_ –

The Dream Keeper

Bring me all of your dreams,

You dreamer,

Bring me all your

Heart melodies

That I may wrap them

In a blue cloud-cloth

Away from the too-rough fingers

Of the world.

Langston Hughes

Tell Me It's A Dream.

By a grove of ash slowly flows a stream,

Following me hauntingly even in dream.

The eddying of water surrounding the stones,

Soothing the aches and pains from out of
my bones.

Mine is a wanting for peace, perfect peace,

I find it here in nature's own sweet masterpiece.

The sounds of rippling waters is music to
my ears,

Washing away all of my imaginary fears.

Warmed by the gentle sun shining on my face,

Watching a spider spinning threads of fine
gossamer lace.

No loud noise to interrupt my reverie so sweet,

Rendezvous with the past, future perhaps
to meet.

Far away the cooing of a turtle dove,

Singing of it's never ending love.

High in the sky the lark in full song,

I am at peace with the world nothing is wrong.

Join me by the ash grove and slow moving
stream,

Listen to Nature, and then tell me it's a dream.

George Bernard Shaw

Dreams

All people dream, but not equally.

Those who dream by night in the dusty recesses
    of their mind,

Wake in the morning to find that it was vanity.

But the dreamers of the day are dangerous people,

For they dream their dreams with open eyes,

And make them come true.

D. H. Lawrence

Like dreaming, reading performs the prodigious task of carrying us off to other worlds. But reading is not dreaming because books, unlike dreams, are subject to our will: they envelop us in alternative realities only because we give them explicit permission to do so. Books are the dreams we would most like to have, and, like dreams, they have the power to change consciousness, turning sadness to laughter and anxious introspection to the relaxed contemplation of some other time and place.

Victor Null

Keep true to the dreams of thy youth.

Friedrich Von Schiller

You may give them your love but not your thoughts.

For they have their own thoughts.

You may house their bodies but not their souls,

For their souls dwell in the house of tomorrow,
   which you cannot visit, not even in your dreams.

Kahlil Gibran

Throw your dream into space like a kite, and you do not know what it will bring back, a new life, a new friend, a new love, a new country.

Dreams pass into the reality of action. From the action stems the dream again; and this interdependence produces the highest form of living.

Anaïs Nin

From The Dream

Our life is twofold; Sleep hath its own world,

A boundary between the things misnamed

Death and existence: Sleep hath its own world,

And a wide realm of wild reality,

And dreams in their development have breath,

And tears, and tortures, and the touch of joy;

They leave a weight upon our waking thoughts,

They take a weight from off waking toils,

They do divide our being; they become

A portion of ourselves as of our time,
And look like heralds of eternity;
They pass like spirits of the past – they speak
Like sibyls of the future; they have power –
The tyranny of pleasure and of pain;
They make us what we were not – what they will,
And shake us with the vision that's gone by,
The dread of vanished shadows – Are they so?
Is not the past all shadow? – What are they?
Creations of the mind? – The mind can make
Substances, and people planets of its own
With beings brighter than have been, and give
A breath to forms which can outlive all flesh.
I would recall a vision which I dreamed
Perchance in sleep – for in itself a thought,
A slumbering thought, is capable of years,
And curdles a long life into one hour.

Lord Byron

He who would interpret a dream must himself be, so to speak, on a level with the dream, for in no single thing can one ever hope to see beyond what one is oneself.

C. G. Jung

Reality can destroy the dream,
why shouldn't the dream destroy reality?

George Moore

A Morning Dream

This morning I dreamed I followed
Widely spaced bells, ringing in the wind,
And climbed through mists to rosy clouds.
I realized my destined affinity
With An Ch'i-sheng the ancient sage.
I met unexpectedly O Lu-hua
The heavenly maiden.

Together we saw lotus roots as big as boats.
Together we ate jujubes as huge as melons.
We were the guests of those on swaying lotus seats.
They spoke in splendid language,
Full of subtle meanings.
They argued with sharp words over paradoxes.
We drank tea brewed on living fire.

Although this might not help the Emperor to govern,
It is endless happiness.
The life of men could be like this.

Why did I have to return to my former home,
Wake up, dress, sit in meditation.
Cover my ears to shut out the disgusting racket.
My heart knows I can never see my dream come true.
At least I can remember
That world and sigh.

Li Ch'ing Chao

Sleep

The breeze at dawn has secrets to tell you.
Don't go back to sleep.

You must ask for what you really want.
Don't go back to sleep.

People are going back and forth
Where the two worlds touch.
The door is round and open.

Don't go back to sleep.

Rumi

The Dog may bark, but the caravan moves on.

Proverb

Art

Fate from an unimaginable throne
Scatters a million roses on the world.
They fall like shooting stars across the sky
Glittering. Under a dark clump of trees
Man, a gaunt creature, squats upon the ground
Apelike, and grins to see those brilliant flowers
Raining through the dark foliage; he tries
Sometimes to clutch at them but in his hands
They melt like snow. Then in despair he turns
Back to his wigwam, stirs the embers, pats
His blear-eyed dog and smokes a pipe, and soon
Wrapp'd in a blanket, drowses off to sleep.

But all his dreams are full of flying flowers.

Vivian de Sola Pinto

The Dream Caravan

Here we are, all of us: in a dream-caravan.
A caravan, but a dream – a dream, but a
    caravan.
And we know which are the dreams.
Therein lies the hope.

Bahaudin, *El Shah*

Life

Tell me not, in mournful numbers,
  Life is but an empty dream!
For the soul is dead that slumbers,
  And things are not what they seem.

Life is real! Life is earnest!
  And the grave is not its goal;
Dust thou art, to dust returnest,
  Was not spoken of the soul.

Henry Wadsworth Longfellow

Dream Truth

The universe is an endless masquerade:
For nothing here is utterly what it seems,
It is a dream-fact vision of a truth
Which but for the dream would not be wholly
    true,
A phenomenon stands out significant
Against dim backgrounds of eternity;
We accept its face and pass by all it means;
A part is seen, we take it for the whole.

Aurobindo

From Dream Pedlary

If there were dreams to sell,
What would you buy?
Some cost a passing bell
Some a light sigh,
That shakes from Life's fresh crown
Only a rose-leaf down.
If there were dreams to sell,
Merry and sad to tell,
And the crier rang the bell,
What would you buy?

A cottage lone and still,
With bowers nigh,
Shadowy, my woes to still,
Until I die.
Such pearl from Life's fresh crown
Fain would I shake me down.
Were dreams to have at will,
This would best heal my ill,
This would I buy.

Thomas Lovell Beddoes

– Enchantment –

Song of Enchantment

A Song of Enchantment I sang me there,
In a green, green wood, by waters fair,
Just as the words came up to me
I sang it under the wild wood tree.

Widdershins turned I, singing it low,
Watching the wild birds come and go;
No cloud in the deep dark blue to be seen
Under the thick-thatched branches green.

Twilight came; silence came;
The planet of Evening's silver flame;
By darkening paths I wandered through
Thickets trembling with drops of dew.

But the music is lost and the words are gone
Of the song I sang as I sat alone,
Ages and ages have fallen on me –
On the wood and the pool and the elder tree.

Walter de la Mare

The Valley Of Enchantment

When a gentle breeze is whisp'ring
in the glamour of the night,
as it brings in ling'ring fragrance
it completes a dream's delight.
Then my thoughts are fondly roving
to a spot I'll always know
in the Valley of Enchantment
it's the place I often go.
When the night is full of splendor
as a bright moon softly gleams,
when the Milky Way is leading
to my sylvan land of dreams,
then it's there I will be heading
for another rendezvous,
in the Valley of Enchantment
where I always am with you.

Peppino Vlannes

What verse is for the poet, dialectical thinking is for the philosopher. He grasps for it in order to get hold of his own enchantment, in order to perpetuate it.

Friedrich Nietzsche

Enchantment

Colored glasses spinning light,
From tulips blooming very bright,
Bedding glorious beauty past,
As you smiled at me so glad

Blessed Grace by the Most High,
Zaphyr flowers opened wide.
Callas lilies graciously stood,
As Shakespeare, rhymed so well!

Skilled artists painting clouds
Perfect strokes filled the skies.
Dogwoods, juniper and hemlocks
Showing nature's souvenirs best

Petals rippening airy and fair
Sunny gates facing winds and sun.
Swaying branches high and low
From the mellowed chestnut trees

Dorian Petersen Potter

From the Snow Queen

Then Gerda told her everything, while the old woman shook her head, and said, 'Hem-hem'; and when she had finished, Gerda asked if she had not seen little Kay, and the old woman told her he had not passed by that way, but he very likely would come. So she told Gerda not to be sorrowful, but to taste the cherries and look at the flowers; they were better than any picture-book, for each of them could tell a story. Then she took Gerda by the hand, and led her into the little house, and the old woman closed the door. The windows were very high, and as the panes were red, blue, and yellow, the daylight shone through them in all sorts of singular colours. On the table stood some beautiful cherries, and Gerda had permission to eat as many as she would. While she was eating them, the old woman combed out her long flaxen ringlets with a golden comb, and the glossy curls hung down on each side of the little round pleasant face, which looked fresh and blooming as a rose. 'I have long been wishing for a dear little maiden like you,' said the old woman, 'and now you must stay with me and see how happily we shall live together.' And while she went on combing little Gerda's hair, she thought less and less about her adopted brother Kay, for the old woman could conjure, although she was not a wicked witch; she conjured only a little for her own amusement, and now, because she wanted to keep Gerda. Therefore she went into the garden, and stretched out her crutch towards all the rose-trees, beautiful though they were, and they immediately sunk into the dark earth, so that no one could tell where they had once stood. The old woman was afraid that if little Gerda saw roses, she would think of those at home, and then remember little Kay, and run away. Then she took Gerda into the flower-garden. How fragrant and beautiful it was! Every flower that could be thought of for every season of the year was here in full bloom; no picture-book could have more beautiful colours. Gerda jumped for joy, and played till the sun went down behind the tall cherry-trees; then she slept in an elegant bed with red silk pillows, embroidered with coloured violets; and then she dreamed as pleasantly as a queen on her wedding-day. The next day, and for many days after, Gerda played with the flowers in the warm sunshine. She knew every flower, and yet, although there were so many of them, it seemed as if one were missing, but which it was she could not tell. One day, however, as she sat looking at the old woman's hat with the painted flowers on it, she saw that the prettiest of them all was a rose. The old woman had forgotten to take it from her hat when she made all the roses sink into the earth. But it is difficult to keep the thoughts together in everything; one little mistake upsets all our arrangements.

'What, are there no roses here?' cried Gerda and she ran out into the garden, and examined all the beds, and searched and searched. There was not one to be found. Then she sat down and wept, and her tears fell just on the place where one of the rose-trees had sunk down. The warm tears moistened the earth, and the rose-tree sprouted up at once, as blooming as when it had sunk; and Gerda embraced it, and kissed the roses, and thought of the beautiful roses at home, and, with them, of little Kay.

Hans Christian Andersen

A Song of Enchantment

the world
poetry in motion
the creator
works
his poem
in the wind
in the breeze
buzz of the bees
chirp of birds
croaks of frogs
hoats of owls
yelps of dogs
london storm
mom's lullabies
the world
a poetry in motion
i am swept
by that
mysterious hand
puppeteers
poet who writes
not in words
but in colours,
cheers, and at times
deep silence

John Tiong Chunghoo

From The King of Elfland's Daughter

When Lirazel looked upon the fields we know, as strange to her as once they had been to us, their beauty delighted her. She laughed to see the haystacks and loved their quaintness. A lark was singing and Lirazel spoke to it, and the lark seemed not to understand, but she turned to other glories of our fields, for all were new to her, and forgot the lark. It was curiously no longer the season of bluebells, for all the foxgloves were blooming and the may was gone and the wild roses were there. Alveric never understood this.

It was early morning and the sun was shining, giving soft colours to our fields, and Lirazel rejoiced in those fields of ours at more common things than one might believe there were amongst the familiar sights of Earth's every day. So glad was she, so gay with her cries of surprise and her laughter, that there seemed thenceforth to Alveric a beauty that he had never dreamed of in buttercups, and a humour in carts that he never had thought of before. Each moment she found with a cry of joyous discovery some treasure of Earth's that he had not known to be fair.

Lord Dunsany

– *Endurance* –

The heights by great men reached and kept
　　Were not attained by sudden flight,
But they, while their companions slept,
　　Were toiling upward in the night.

Henry Wadsworth Longfellow

What can't be cured, must be endured.

Proverb

Nothing happens to any man that he is not formed
by nature to bear.

Marcus Aurelius

… we could never learn to be brave and patient,
if there were only joy in the world.

Helen Keller

Job endured everything – until his friends came to
comfort him, then he grew impatient.

Soren Kierkegaard

Endurance

With all the infinite possibilities of spiritual life before you, do not settle down on a little patch of dusty ground at the mountain's foot in restful content. Be not content until you reach the mountain's summit.

J. R. Miller

Does the road wind up-hill all the way?
Yes, to the very end.
Will the day's journey take the whole long day?
From morn to night, my friend.

Christina Rossetti

Let's talk sense to the American people. Let's tell them the truth, that there are no gains without pains.

Adlai Stevenson

If you can't stand the heat, get out of the kitchen.

Harry S. Truman

Maybe one day we shall be glad to remember even these hardships.

Virgil

– *Faith* –

Faith Will Come

You say you have no faith?
Love – and faith will come.
You say you are sad?
Love – and joy will come.
You say you are alone?
Love – and you will break out of your solitude.
You say you are in hell?
Love – and you will find yourself in heaven.

Carlo Carretto

The Eye of Faith

The eye of Faith can always see the gold beyond the grey –
though the gleam be distant and the glory far away … The
eye of Doubt with vision blurred looks out into the night –
and sees no promise of the dawn, no glimmering of light.

The eye of Faith can pierce the gloom of grief and tragedy –
and through the shadows can behold God's boundless charity.

Anon

Invictus

Out of the night that covers me,
Black as the pit from pole to pole,
I thank whatever gods may be,
For my unconquerable soul.

In the fell clutch of circumstance,
I have winced but not cried aloud.
Under the bludgeonings of chance,
My head is bloodied but unbowed.

Beyond this place of wrath and tears,
Looms but the horror of the shade.
And yet the menace of the years,
Finds, and shall find me, unafraid.

It matters not how strait the gate.
How charged with punishments
      the scroll,
I am the master of my fate,
I am the captain of my soul.

William Ernest Henley *Great Discoveries*

I Believe in the deep blue sky and the smiling water. I can see through the clouds of the sky and am not afraid of the waves of the sea.

I Believe in the loving friendships given by the flowers and the trees. Outwardly they die but in the heart they live forever. Little paths through the woods I love, and the sound of leaves on the ground or of a nut falling or even of a broken twig.

I Believe that the days to come already feel the wonder of the days that are passed and will permit the wonder to endure and increase.

I Believe in and love my belief in, and my love for, all these things and most of all, I believe in and love the Source of my belief and love.

Ancient Chinese Tradition

Courage and Faith

As the essence of courage is to stake one's life on a possibility, so the essence of faith is to believe that the possibility exists.

William Salter

The Man Without Faith

A man without faith
Grows old before his years,
His world a wraith,
For whom the end nears
Like a winter mist
When the sun is cold
In the cold west.

His children about him
Are strangers, unknown;
The love that begot them
Cooled and gone.

If he get riches
They turn to rust,
And he can do nothing
With a handful of dust.
Life's miracle fails him,
Life's rapture, life's breath;
He has done with living,
He has forestalled death.

Richard Church

Life's Journey

Sometime in your life you will go on a journey. It will be the longest journey you have ever taken. It is the journey to find yourself.

Katherine Sharp

I Am

I know not whence I came,
I know not whither I go
But the fact stands clear that I am here
In this world of pleasure and woe.
And out of the mist and murk,
Another truth shines plain.
It is in my power each day and hour
To add to its joy or its pain.

I know that the earth exists,
It is none of my business why.
I cannot find out what it's all about,
I would but waste time to try.
My life is a brief, brief thing,
I am here for a little space.
And while I stay I would like, if I may,
To brighten and better the place.

The trouble, I think, with us all
Is the lack of a high conceit.
If each man thought he was sent to
    this spot
To make it a bit more sweet,
How soon we could gladden the world,
How easily right all wrong.
If nobody shirked, and each one worked
To help his fellows along.

Cease wondering why you came –
Stop looking for faults and flaws.
Rise up today in your pride and say,
'I am part of the First Great Cause!
However full the world
There is room for an earnest man.
It had need of me or I would not be,
I am here to strengthen the plan.'

Ella Wheeler Wilcox

Faith

Faith is like a boomerang; begin using what you have
and it comes back to you in greater measure.

Charles L. Allen

I Asked God

I asked God to take away my pain.
God said, No.
It is not for me to take away,
but for you to give it up.

I asked God to make my handicapped child whole.
God said, No.
His spirit is whole,
his body is only temporary.

I asked God to grant me patience.
God said, No.
Patience is a by-product of tribulations;
it isn't granted, it is learned.

I asked God to give me happiness.
God said, No.
I give you blessings.
Happiness is up to you.

I asked God to spare me pain.
God said, No.
Suffering draws you apart from worldly cares
and brings you closer to me.

I asked God to make my spirit grow.
God said, No.
You must grow on your own,
but I will prune you to make you fruitful.

I asked God for all things that I might enjoy life.
God said, No.
I will give you life,
so that you may enjoy all things.

I asked God to help me love others, as much as
  He loves me.
God said … Ahhh, finally you have the idea.

Anon

Supreme Faith

The person who has a firm trust in the Supreme Being
is powerful in his power, wise by his wisdom, happy
by his happiness.

Joseph Addison

– *Fantasy* –

Fantasy

It may indeed be fantasy when I
Essay to draw from all created things
Deep, heartfelt, inward joy that closely clings;
And trace in leaves and flowers that round me lie
Lessons of love and earnest piety.
So let it be; and if the wide world rings
In mock of this belief, it brings
Nor fear, nor grief, nor vain perplexity.
So will I build my altar in the fields,
And the blue sky my fretted dome shall be,
And the sweet fragrance that the wild flower yields
Shall be the incense I will yield to Thee,
Thee only God! and thou shalt not despise
Even me, the priest of this poor sacrifice.

Samuel Taylor Coleridge

The true nature of things, truth itself, can be revealed to us
only by fantasy, which is more realistic than all the realisms.

Eugène Ionesco

Fantasy

I saw a peacock with a fiery tail,
I saw a blazing comet drop down hail,
I saw a cloud wrapped with ivy round,
I saw an oak creep upon the ground,
I saw a pismire swallow up a whale,
I saw the sea brimful of ale,
I saw a Venice glass full fifteen feet deep,
I saw a well full of men's tears that weep,
I saw red eyes all of a flaming fire,
I saw a house bigger than the moon and higher,
I saw the sun at twelve o'clock at night,
I saw the man that saw this wondrous sight.

Anon.

The King who wanted to touch the Moon

There was once a King who had an idea and one idea only. He wanted to touch the moon. He thought and thought how he could do this. In fact he could think of nothing else. Instead of attending to the affairs of state, he thought up plans which would help him to achieve his fantastic ambitions. He'd lie awake all night trying to solve the problem and when he slept he dreamt about it.

One day he called his Head Carpenter and said: 'I'm determined to touch the moon, so you must build me a tower that will reach up to the sky. After that, we'll see what we shall see.'

The Carpenter was afraid to tell the King that such a tower was impossible. He would have to build it with wood. That was the only material he had and there was not enough of it in the royal workshops. So he pretended to make plans, bustling about with his drawing-board and tools.

Weeks passed and nothing happened. The King became impatient and irritable and sent for his Head Carpenter.

'If you haven't built my tower in three days, I'll have your head chopped off!' he roared.

Again the Carpenter bustled about, hammer in hand, not knowing what to do. One day passed. Then another, but on the third day the Carpenter had an idea and he went to see the King.

'Work on the tower has been held up, Your Majesty,' the Carpenter said. 'I have studied the problem from every angle. I see now how it can be done. I want you to order everyone to bring boxes and crates to the palace grounds. This will give me the necessary material.'

So the King ordered everyone to bring all the boxes and crates they could find to the palace grounds and, under the Head Carpenter's directions, they were piled one on top of the other until there wasn't a single box or crate left.

'It's not high enough,' complained the King when he saw the tower. And he ordered all the trees to be chopped down and sawn up into planks to make more boxes.

At last every tree had been felled, and every tree trunk had been sawn into planks and every plank had been made into a box, and every box had been piled on top of the tower. It was now a very high tower.

'I'll climb the tower first to make sure it's safe,' the Carpenter said.

'You'll do nothing of the sort,' the King said indignantly. 'I shall make the first ascent. Whoever heard of a carpenter rising to such heights?'

Then the King began to climb.

He climbed and climbed to the very top and he stretched out his hand to reach the moon. Only a few more inches and he would be able to reach it. 'Bring me up one more box!' he called to his Carpenter below.

There wasn't another box to be found anywhere. Nor was there a scrap of wood to make one. There wasn't a single tree left in the whole land, they had all been cut down.

The King was furious. He was so near and yet so far from touching the moon. Yet he must succeed. Then he had a brilliant idea.

'Take the box from the bottom of the tower and bring it up here to me!' he ordered.

'What, the *first* one?' asked the carpenters in astonishment. (They were so put out, they forgot to add 'Your Majesty'.) 'The box on which all the others are piled?'

'Of course, you dolts!' roared the King, 'and be quick about it or you'll all lose your heads!'

The carpenters looked at each other in dismay. The King's orders were law and they were loyal subjects. So, when the King shouted his commands a second time, they hesitated no longer and pulled out the bottom box, as he had ordered.

You can imagine what happened. Down came the King's tower and somewhere under the hundreds and thousands of boxes was the King. No one knows if he was ever found, but they do know he never touched the moon.

West Indian Folk Tale

It is far harder to kill a phantom than a reality.

Virginia Woolf

– *Friendship* –

True Friendship

True friendship is a plant of slow growth and must undergo and withstand the shocks of adversity before it is entitled to the appellation.

George Washington

If a man does not make new acquaintance as he advances through life, he will soon find himself left alone. A man, Sir, should keep his friendship in constant repair.

Samuel Johnson

Love And Friendship

Oh, the comfort, the inexpressible comfort
of feeling safe with a person;
having neither to weigh thoughts nor measure
   words,
but pour them all out, just as they are,
chaff and grain together,
Knowing that a faithful hand will take and
   sift them,
keep what is worth keeping,
And then with the breath of kindness,
   blow the rest away.

George Eliot

The only way to have a friend is to be one.

Ralph Waldo Emerson

Books and friends should be few but good.

Proverb

Tell me what company thou keeps
and I'll tell thee what thou are.

Miguel de Cervantes

You Needed Me

I cried a tear, you wiped it dry,
I was confused, you cleared my mind,
I sold my soul, you bought it back for me,
You held me up and gave me dignity,
Somehow you needed me.

You gave me strength to stand alone again
To face the world out on my own again...

You held my hand when it was cold,
When I was lost you took me home,
You gave me hope when I was at the end
And turned my lies back into truth again,
You even called me 'Friend'.

Randy Goodrum

Have no friends not equal to yourself.

Confucius

Forsake not an old friend; for the new is not comparable to him: a new friend is as new wine; when it is old, thou shalt drink it with pleasure.

Ecclesiasticus

A Friend may well be reckoned
the masterpiece of Nature.

Ralph Waldo Emerson

Changez vos amis.
Change your friends.

Charles De Gaulle

I get by with a little help from my friends.

John Lennon

Friendship

We cannot tell the precise moment when friendship is formed. As in filling a vessel drop by drop, there is at last a drop which makes it run over; so in a series of kindnesses there is at last one which makes the heart run over.

Samuel Johnson

Associate yourself with men of good quality if you esteem your own reputation; for 'tis better to be alone than in bad company.

George Washington

Make Worthy Friends

Your friends are your larger family. From among them one chooses wife or husband, business and professional associates. Wide friendships enrich character. Form a few selected friends among people wiser than you. In youth have friends among older people; in later years, young friends. Youth has need of age and age has need of youth. Choose your friends with care. Prefer people for what they are, not what they have. One tends to become like his friends and to be judged by them. Avoid attaching to yourself as friends persons who are intemperate, avaricious, extravagant, or ungrateful. Our friends are a part of our larger selves. We identify ourselves with their happiness and seek to be worthy of their friendship. These higher loyalties make life significant. They ennoble life and furnish comfort and happy memories for our later years.

Anon

Fate chooses your relations, you choose your friends.

Jacques Delille

Saul and Jonathan were lovely and pleasant in their lives, and in their death they were not divided: they were swifter than eagles, they were stronger than lions.

Samuel

Two may talk together under the same roof for many years, yet never really meet; and two others at first speech are old friends.

Mary Catherwood

To like and dislike the same things,
that is indeed true friendship.

Sallust

The best of friends must part.

Proverb

There is no such thing as a free lunch.

Milton Friedman

It is not so much our friends' help that helps us as the confident knowledge that they will help us.

Epicurus

A woman can become a man's friend only in the following stages – first an acquaintance, next a mistress, and only then a friend.

Anton Chekhov

Without My Friends the Day is Dark

What harm have I done to the stars?

On the night that my friends
foregather with me,

They fly quickly, like birds,
from the face of the sky;

But on the nights that I sit in
loneliness,

They limp, as though they were
too weary to move.

Without my friends the day
is dark,

But in their company the night is
luminous.

Moses Ibn Ezra

Always, Sir, set a high value on spontaneous kindness. He whose inclination prompts him to cultivate your friendship of his own accord, will love you more than one whom you have been at pains to attach to you.

Samuel Johnson

Friendship is unnecessary, like philosophy, like art … It has
no survival value; rather it is one of those things that give
value to survival.

C. S. Lewis

The Arrow And The Song

I shot an arrow into the air,
It fell to earth, I knew not where;
For, so swiftly it flew, the sight
Could not follow it in its flight.

I breathed a song into the air,
It fell to earth, I knew not where;
For who has sight so keen and strong,
That it can follow the flight of song?

Long, long afterward, in an oak
I found the arrow, still unbroke;
And the song, from beginning to end,
I found again in the heart of a friend.

Henry Wadsworth Longfellow

Love is blind; friendship closes its eyes.

Proverb

A true bond of friendship is usually only possible between people of roughly equal status. This equality is demonstrated in many indirect ways, but it is reinforced in face-to-face encounters by a matching of the posture of relaxation or alertness.

Desmond Morris

Equality

Be the same to your friends whether in
prosperity or adversity.

Periander

– *Gardens* –

God Almighty first planted a garden.
And indeed it is the purest of human pleasures.

Francis Bacon

To get the best results you must talk to your vegetables.

Charles, Prince of Wales

Oh, Adam was a gardener, and God who made
    him sees

That half a proper gardener's work is done upon
    his knees,

So when your work is finished, you can wash
    your hands and pray

For the Glory of the Garden, that it may not
    pass away!

Rudyard Kipling

A Blind Girl in the Orchard

Everything that could hum, or buzz, or sing, or bloom, had
a part in my education – noisy-throated frogs, katydids and
crickets held in my hand until, forgetting their embarrass-
ment, they trilled their reedy note, little downy chickens
and wildflowers, the dogwood blossoms, meadow-violets
and budding fruit trees. I felt the bursting cotton-balls and
fingered their soft fibre and fuzzy seeds; I felt the low
soughing of the wind through the cornstalks, the silky
rustling of the long eaves, and the indignant snort of my
pony, as we caught him in the pasture and put the bit in his
mouth – ah me! how well I remember the spicy, clovery
smell of his breath!

Sometimes I rose at dawn and stole into the garden while
the heavy dew lay on the grass and flowers. Few know what
joy it is to feel the roses pressing softly into the hand, or the
beautiful motion of the lilies as they sway in the morning

breeze. Sometimes I caught an insect in the flower I was plucking, and I felt the faint noise of a pair of wings rubbed together in a sudden terror, as the little creature became aware of a pressure from without.

Another favourite haunt of mine was the orchard, where the fruit ripened early in July. The large, downy peaches would reach themselves into my hand, and as the joyous breezes flew about the trees the apples tumbled at my feet. Oh, the delight with which I gathered up the fruit in my pinafore, pressed my face against the smooth cheeks of the apples, still warm from the sun, and skipped back to the house!

Helen Keller, *The Story of My Life*, 1903

Not Wholly in the Busy World

Not wholly in the busy world, nor quite
Beyond it, blooms the garden that I love.
News from the humming city comes to it
In sound of funeral or of marriage bells;
And, sitting muffled in dark leaves, you hear
The windy clanging of the minster clock;
Although between it and the garden lies
A league of grass, wash'd by a slow broad stream,
That, stirr'd with languid pulses of the oar,
Waves all its lazy lilies, and creeps on,
Barge-laden, to three arches of a bridge
Crown' d with the minster-towers.

The fields between
Are dewy-fresh, browsed by deep-udder'd kine,
And all about the large lime feathers low,
The lime a summer home of murmurous wings.

Alfred Lord Tennyson

The Glory of the Garden

June

June is the month of sweet scents. *Philadelphus* or syringa as it is generally called burdens the air with its heavy perfume. The dark red sweet-williams offer their own homely and unsophisticated fragrance; that of the pansies, although less obvious, is intimate and refined. The viola, unlike the stocks, does not broadcast her scent over the whole garden; she withholds it, reserving her secret sweetness for those who seek it and not for the casual passer-by. An odour of sanctity clings about the Madonna lilies as they stand nun-like under the arches of the trees. Roses swing their thuribles, and the fumes from the incense burning at their hearts come and go upon the vagrant airs. June is indeed a vendor of perfumes, but in spite of the wide varieties of scent that she has to offer, there are many who think that the sweetest is that of the old favourite, Mrs. Sinkins, the double white pink. The winding path that twists between the rhododendrons and the lilies is edged on either side by these old-fashioned pinks and the pungent fragrance that is now hanging about that part of the garden is overpowering. The sun came out today after a brief shower and the sudden waves of heat beating upon the wet flowers seemed to draw every vestige of scent out of them. It is a great pity that they do not have a longer life, but the silvery-grey foliage is pretty all the year round and if cut the flowers last a long time, sending out their sweetness into every corner of the house.

The carnations also lend their rich scent to the June winds, but I lament the passing of the old crimson clove. It seems to have been left behind in the ceaseless search for bigger and better blooms; this dark velvety beauty is surely the loveliest of the whole dianthus family. It is not surprising that the Greeks called the carnation, Divine Flower.

December

The flocking of birds is one of the most fascinating things to watch when you are seated at an upstairs window looking out upon your winter garden. Great whirling clouds of wings move out across the sky as if impelled by the impulse of a single brain. How do those large companies of birds keep together in disciplined formation? Do they have leaders, and if so how are they appointed? At what signal does the flock rise from the ground and fly undirected to a particular point? To watch a vast flock of birds swinging out upon the wind is to experience a faint spasm of the ecstasy with which these winged creatures go soaring up into the blue. A bird is the living embodiment of the spirit of freedom. Sing it must, because by its very nature a bird is a thing of joy. Something of the mass ecstasy of the flock can be sensed by the watcher at the window, but only those who have dived into the sea and cleaved deep water with the clean swift movements of their own naked limbs can come near to understanding the rapture that must possess the birds as they plunge breast forward from the tops of the trees. The diver, like the bird, flings himself into space, gliding gracefully down the precipitous slopes of the air.

Yesterday evening a skein of wild geese passed over the garden, flying in perfect formation with their long necks extended and their great wings beating the air. They seemed to be flying low, not much higher than the poplars. No doubt they were making for new feeding grounds, possibly the mud flats about the creeks and saltings of the tidal harbour ten miles away. It was an amazing spectacle. Those geese knew where they were going. There was a single-minded purposefulness about that flight. How did they know the way to the creeks? By what magical means did they keep on their course? More mysteries. More unanswered and unanswerable questions.

Anon

God the first garden made, and the first city Cain.

Abraham Cowley

Gardening Involves You in the Cycle of Life

Whether you grow something from seed or merely clip a perennial shrub, the contact with the wonders of the natural world will lift your spirits and the workings of Mother Nature will never cease to amaze you.

Anon

Hyacinth

When the blue, proud Hyancinth dies, he falls
slowly inward; flower fading crinkles
first, and then his tips of tall green spears
turning gold, begin to burn.

The bulb of his own Self Light
that hides, until a Spring to come
in darkest soil, is drinking him,
all of him up, O Lord of Caves!

Let his sapphire die back into earth
and then, consumed
in your fire, spring forth!
O Lord of the River and of Caves.

Jane Adams

Three Garden Poems

You are a Sunny Garden
You are a sunny garden,
a very flowering place
where autumn's sun is stayed
to tangle with your hair.

Now berry-fall is turned
to lark-rise as you walk,
and summer's flowers
distilled so in your smile,

that wealth beyond compare
is but to stand and stare.

Husbandman
Husbandman,
till the soil and comb the shining hair,
harrow and kiss
and plant your seed in mellow soil
or deep within the warm and longing flesh.
The crop of barley and the crop of children
will shine in the single sun
and blow to the same wind.
Their time will be of flowering,
of fruiting and of fall.

Together breathing, see the barley feed the
    children
and the children point to grow the corn.

Question and Answer

Gardener, what are you digging
    in your plot of dark earth?

I am ploughing my body
    that it may be healthy and strong.

Fool, why do you stand out there in the rain,
    your hair plastered about your face?

I am listening to my blood
    falling so gently from heaven.

Brother, come into the house.
When the wind is howling,
    why do you stand on the hilltop
    your arms outspread?

I am embracing my song
    before it is uttered.

Peter Adams

The Rose

O Rose, thou flower of flowers, thou fragrant wonder,
Who shall describe thee in thy ruddy prime,
Thy perfect fullness in the summer-time,
When the pale leaves blushingly part asunder
And show the warm red heart lies glowing under!
Thou should'st bloom surely in some sunny clime,
Untouched by blights and chilly winter's rime,
Where lightnings never flash nor peals the thunder.
And yet in happier spheres they cannot need thee
So much as we do with our weight of woe;
Perhaps they would not tend, perhaps not heed thee,
And thou wouldst lonely and neglected grow;
And He who is all wise, He hath decreed thee
To gladden earth and cheer all hearts below.

Christina Rossetti

The kiss of sun for pardon,
The song of the birds for mirth –
One is nearer God's Heart in a garden
Than anywhere else on earth.

Dorothy Gurney

- *Happiness* -

Any Morning

Just lying on the couch and being happy.
Only humming a little, the quiet sound in the head.
Trouble is busy elsewhere at the moment, it has
so much to do in the world.

People who might judge are mostly asleep; they can't
monitor you all the time, and sometimes they forget.
When dawn flows over the hedge you can
get up and act busy.

Little corners like this, pieces of Heaven
left lying around, can be picked up and saved.
People won't even see that you have them,
they are so light and easy to hide.

Later in the day you can act like the others.
You can shake your head. You can frown.

William Stafford

One joy scatters a hundred griefs.

Chinese proverb

Yes

I thank God for most this amazing
day; for the leaping greenly spirits of trees
and a blue true dream of sky; and for everything
which is natural, which is infinite, which is yes.

E.E. Cummings

That action is best,
which procures the greatest happiness
for the greatest numbers.

Francis Hutcheson

We are never so happy nor so unhappy as we imagine.

Duc de la Rochefoucauld

Not in Utopia, subterranean fields,
Or some secreted island, Heaven knows where!
But in the very world, which is the world
Of all of us, – the place where, in the end,
We find our happiness, or not at all!

William Wordsworth

To Be Happy

to be happy

help

help someone

help someone who needs it

help someone who needs it badly

help someone who needs it badly and you know
there will be no return

help someone who is not related to you

help someone who is not your close friend

help someone who does not expect you to

help when it is not your duty

help in whatever way you can

help

and you will be happy

Anon

If you haven't been happy very young, you can still be
happy later on, but it's much harder. You need more luck.

Simone de Beauvoir

Happiness is a mystery like religion,
and should never be rationalized.

G. K. Chesterton

There was a jolly miller once,
Lived on the river Dee;
He worked and sang from morn till night;
No lark more blithe than he.

Isaac Bickerstaffe

When the green woods laugh with the voice of joy.

William Blake

Happiness is like coke – something you get as a by-product in the process of making something else.

Aldous Huxley

Ask yourself whether you are happy,
and you cease to be so.

John Stuart Mill

When a small child ... I thought that success spelled happiness. I was wrong. Happiness is like a butterfly which appears and delights us for one brief moment, but soon flits away.

Anna Pavlova

Life Is For Living

Life is for living so live it and see
what a thrilling and wonderful world it can be
when you let go of the things that annoy
and start to discover the secret of joy;
life is too good to be squandered, too brief
to waste upon grievances, grudges and grief.
Life is for giving, so give of your best.
Keep nothing back and your days will be blessed …
Give time and give money, give thanks and give praise
It will return in mysterious ways.
Life was not meant to depress or destroy.
Life is for giving and giving is joy.

Patience Strong

And we suddenly know, what heaven we're in,
When they begin the beguine.

Cole Porter

Every time I talk to a savant I feel quite sure that happiness
is no longer a possibility. Yet when I talk with my gardener,
I'm convinced of the opposite.

Bertrand Russell

One is happy as a result of one's own efforts, once one knows the necessary ingredients of happiness – simple tastes, a certain degree of courage, self denial to a point, love of work, and, above all, a clear conscience. Happiness is no vague dream, of that I now feel certain.

George Sand

Contentment

Contentment comes as the result of great acceptances and great humilities, of surrendering ourselves to the fullness of life, of letting life flow through us.

David Grayson

Don't Look Back

Do not look back on happiness, or dream of it in the future. You are sure of today. Do not let yourself be cheated out of it.

Anon

Anger

For every minute you are angry
you lose sixty seconds of happiness.

Ralph Waldo Emerson

Happiness

The grand essentials of happiness are – something to do,
something to love and something to hope for.

Allan K. Chambers

Living In The Now

I have the happiness of the passing moment,
and what more can a mortal ask?

George Gissing

Just Be

By being happy we sow anonymous benefits
upon the world.

Robert Louis Stevenson

Prayer

Give me a sense of humor, Lord;
Give me the grace to see a joke,
To get some happiness from life,
And pass it on to other folk.

Chester Cathedral

Happy Days

Make the most of happy days

 for Sorrow comes to all

Make the most of happy days, before the shadows fall

Days of youth, and careless joys before Life makes its
claim

Live each moment, for it's all a glad and glorious
game. . . .

Do not say one word to mar the perfect memory

Live and laugh and love, and then whatever is to be

You'll gather lovely memories into your heart's green
bowers

and live your yesterdays again with all their golden
hours. . . .

And when old age has bound you to a lonely fireside
chair

within your soul there'll always be the echo of a prayer

For as you sit there quietly dreaming in the autumn haze

You'll fold your hands, and say

'Thank God, for all my happy days.'

Patience Strong

Nothing else in the world can make man unhappy but fear.
The misfortune we suffer is seldom if ever as bad as that
which we fear.

Schiller

Emptying The Guest Room

Where is my depression gone?
It has to have a room
somewhere inside this house:
a place, which I can peep at from my hole,
each time my mind has changed me to a mouse.

But somehow, now,
depression has become
a mouse-sized room
with less of substance left inside
than rags of shroud,
when all that was alive
has broken out to dance
inside this air,
which wipes out dust and formulas,
to leave the blackboard bare.

Kevan Myers

Acceptance

I accept life unconditionally. Life holds so much – so much
to be so happy about always. Most people ask for happiness
on condition. Happiness can be felt only if you don't
set conditions.

Artur Rubinstein

The Silver Lining

The inner half of every cloud
Is bright and shining;
I therefore turn my clouds about,
And always wear them inside out
To show the lining.

Ellen Thorneycroft Fowler

Source of Happiness

So much unhappiness, it seems to me, is due to nerves; and bad nerves are the result of having nothing to do, or doing a thing badly, unsuccessfully or incompetently. Of all the unhappy people in the world, the unhappiest are those who have not found something they want to do. True happiness comes to him who does his work well, followed by a relaxing and refreshing period of rest. True happiness comes from the right amount of work for the day.

Lin Yutang

Happiness is nothing more than good health
and a bad memory.

Dr Albert Schweitzer

– *Humour* –

After being turned down by numerous publishers,
he decided to write for posterity.

George Ade

What's the first excellence in a lawyer? Tautology.
What the second? Tautology. What the third? Tautology.

Richard Steele

The very last speech she made, half a minute before she
died, was 'See master's under-pants be put to the fire'. She
perished with them beautiful words on her lips.

Eden Phillpotts

Choosing between two candidates, a member of the
Admiralty Board would ask suddenly, 'What was the
number of the taxi you came in?' A candidate who said,
truthfully, 'I don't know' was rejected, and the candidate
who said (lying) 'Number 2351' was promptly admitted as a
boy with initiative.

C. Northcote Parkinson

The Night the Bed Fell In

I suppose that the high-water mark of my youth in Columbus, Ohio, was the night the bed fell on my father. It makes a better recitation (unless, as some friends of mine have said, one has heard it five or six times) than it does a piece of writing, for it is almost necessary to throw furniture around, shake doors, and bark like a dog, to lend the proper atmosphere and verisimilitude to what is admittedly a somewhat incredible tale. Still, it did take place.

It happened, then, that my father had decided to sleep in the attic one night, to be away where he could think. My mother opposed the notion strongly because, she said, the old wooden bed up there was unsafe; it was wobbly and the heavy headboard would crash down on Father's head if the bed fell, and kill him. There was no dissuading him, however, and at a quarter past ten he closed the attic door behind him and went up the narrow twisting stairs. We later heard ominous creakings as he crawled into bed. Grandfather, who usually slept in the attic bed when he was with us, had disappeared some days before. (On these occasions he was usually gone six or eight days and returned growling and out of temper, with the news that the Federal Union was run by a passel of blockheads and that the Army of the Potomac didn't have any more chance than a fiddler's bitch.)

We had visiting us at this time a nervous first cousin of mine named Briggs Beall, who believed that he was likely to cease breathing when he was asleep. It was his feeling that if he were not awakened every hour during the night, he might die of suffocation. He had been accustomed to setting an alarm clock to ring at intervals until morning, but I persuaded him to abandon this. He slept in my room and I told him that I was such a light sleeper that if anybody quit breathing in the same room with me, I would wake instantly. He tested me the first night – which I had suspected he would – by holding his breath after my regular breathing had convinced him I was asleep. I was not asleep, however, and called to him. This seemed to allay his fears a little, but he took the precaution of putting a glass of spirits of camphor on a little table at the head of his bed. In case I didn't arouse him until he was almost gone, he said, he would sniff the camphor, a powerful reviver. Briggs was not the only member of his family who had his crotchets. Old Aunt Melissa Beall (who could whistle like a man, with two fingers in her mouth) suffered under the premonition that she was destined to die on South High Street, because she had been born on South High Street and married on South High Street. Then there was Aunt Sarah Shoaf, who never went to bed at night without the fear that a burglar was going to get in and blow chloroform under her door through a tube. To avert this calamity – for she was in greater dread of anaesthetics than of losing her household goods – she always piled her money, silverware, and other valuables in a neat stack just outside her bedroom, with a note reading: 'This is all I have. Please take it and do not use your chloroform, as this is all I have.' Aunt Gracie Shoaf also had a burglar phobia, but she met it with more fortitude. She was confident that burglars had been getting into her house every night for forty years. The fact that she never missed anything was to her no proof to the contrary. She always claimed that she scared them off before they could take anything, by throwing shoes down the hallway. When she went to bed she piled, where she could get at them handily, all the shoes there were about her house. Five minutes after she had turned off the light, she would sit up in bed and say 'Hark!' Her husband, who had learned to ignore the whole situation as long ago as 1903, would either be sound asleep or pretend to be sound asleep. In either case he would not respond to her tugging and pulling, so that presently she would arise, tiptoe to the door, open it slightly and heave a shoe down the hall in one direction, and its mate down the hall in the other direction. Some nights she threw them all, some nights only a couple of pairs.

But I am straying from the remarkable incidents that took place during the night that the bed fell on Father. By midnight we were all in bed. The layout of the rooms and the disposition of their occupants is important to an understanding of what later occurred. In the front room upstairs (just under Father's attic bedroom) were my mother and my brother Herman, who sometimes sang in his sleep, usually 'Marching Through Georgia' or 'Onward, Christian Soldiers'. Briggs Beall and myself were in a room adjoining this one. My brother Roy was in a room across the hall from ours. Our bull terrier, Rex, slept in the hall.

My bed was an army cot, one of those affairs which are made wide enough to sleep on comfortably only by putting up, flat with the middle section, the two sides which ordinarily hang down like the sideboards of a drop-leaf table. When these sides are up, it is perilous to roll too far towards the edge, for then the cot is likely to tip completely over, bringing the whole bed down on top of one, with a tremendous banging crash. This, in fact, is precisely what happened, about two o'clock in the morning. (It was my mother who, in recalling the scene later, first referred to it as 'the night the bed fell on your father'.)

Always a deep sleeper, slow to arouse (I had lied to Briggs), I was at first unconscious of what had happened when the iron cot rolled me on to the floor and toppled over on me. It left me still warmly bundled up and unhurt, for the bed rested above me like a canopy. Hence I did not wake up, only reached the edge of consciousness and went back. The racket, however, instantly awakened my mother, in the next room, who came to the immediate conclusion that her worst dread was realized: the big wooden bed upstairs had fallen on Father. She therefore screamed, 'Let's go to your poor father!' It was this shout, rather than the noise of my cot falling, that awakened Herman, in the same room with her. He thought that Mother had become, for no apparent reason, hysterical. 'You're all right, Mamma!' he shouted, trying to calm her. They exchanged shout for shout for perhaps ten seconds: 'Let's go to your poor father!' and 'You're all right!' That woke up Briggs. By this time I was conscious of what was going on, in a vague way, but did not yet realize that I was under my bed instead of on it. Briggs, awakening in the midst of loud shouts of fear and apprehension, came to the quick conclusion that he was suffocating and that we were all trying to 'bring him out'. With a low moan, he grasped the glass of camphor at the head of his bed and instead of sniffing it poured it over himself. The room reeked of camphor. 'Ugf, ahgf,' choked Briggs, like a drowning man, for he had almost succeeded in stopping his breath under the deluge of pungent spirits. He leaped out of bed and groped towards the open window, but he came up against one that was closed. With his hand, he beat out the glass, and I could hear it crash and tinkle on the alleyway below. It was at this juncture that I, in trying to get up, had the uncanny sensation of feeling my bed above me! Foggy with sleep, I now suspected, in my turn, that the whole uproar was being made in a frantic endeavour to extricate me from what must be an unheard-of and perilous situation. 'Get me out of this!' I bawled. 'Get me out!' I think I had the nightmarish belief that I was entombed in a mine. 'Gugh!' gasped Briggs, floundering in his camphor.

By this time my mother, still shouting, pursued by Herman, still shouting, was trying to open the door to the attic, in order to go up and get my father's body out of the wreckage. The door was stuck, however, and wouldn't yield. Her frantic pulls on it only added to the general banging and confusion. Roy and the dog were now up, the one shouting questions, the other barking.

Father, farthest away and soundest sleeper of all, had by this time been awakened by the battering on the attic door. He decided that the house was on fire. 'I'm coming, I'm coming!' he wailed in a slow, sleepy voice – it took him many minutes to regain full consciousness. My mother, still believing he was caught under the bed, detected in his 'I'm coming!' the mournful, resigned note of one who is preparing to meet his Maker. 'He's dying!' she shouted.

'I'm all right!' Briggs yelled to reassure her. 'I'm all right!' He still believed that it was his own closeness to death that was worrying Mother. I found at last the light switch in my room, unlocked the door, and Briggs and I joined the others at the attic door. The dog, who never did like Briggs, jumped for him – assuming that he was the culprit in whatever was going on – and Roy had to throw Rex and hold him. We could hear Father crawling out of bed upstairs. Roy pulled the attic door open, with a mighty jerk, and Father came down the stairs, sleepy and irritable but safe and sound. My mother began to weep when she saw him. Rex began to howl. 'What in the name of God is going on here?' asked Father.

The situation was finally put together like a gigantic jigsaw puzzle. Father caught a cold from prowling around in his bare feet but there were no other bad results. 'I'm glad,' said Mother, who always looked on the bright side of things, 'that your grandfather wasn't here.'

James Thurber

It is very vulgar to talk like a dentist when one isn't a dentist. It produces a false impression.

Oscar Wilde

Keeping a bar is much better than writing a book. Many an English writer has wished he kept a pub instead of a publisher.

G. K. Chesterton

When you sit with a nice girl for two hours, you think it's only a minute. But when you sit on a hot stove for a minute, you think it's two hours. That's relativity.

Albert Einstein

The guy who invented the first wheel was an idiot. The guy who invented the other three, he was the genius.

Sid Caesar

When children are born they bring light into your life. Thereafter they just leave lights on around the house.

Dave Greenhead

A celebrity is a person who works hard all his life to become well-known, then wears dark glasses to avoid being recognized.

Fred Allen

A Fishing Song

There was a boy whose name was Phinn,
    And he was fond of fishing;
His father could not keep him in,
    Nor all his mother's wishing.

His life's ambition was to land
    A fish of several pound weight;
The chief thing he could understand,
    Was hooks, or worms for ground-bait.

The worms crept out, the worms crept in,
    From every crack and pocket;
He had a worm-box made of tin,
    With proper worms to stock it.

He gave his mind to breeding worms
    As much as he was able;
His sister spoke in angry terms
    To see them on the table.

You found one walking up the stairs,
    You found one in a bonnet,
Or, in the bedroom, unawares,
    You set your foot upon it.

Anon

When I was a boy of fourteen, my father was so ignorant I could hardly stand to have the old man around.

But when I got to be twenty-one, I was astonished at how much he had learned in seven years.

Mark Twain

You don't need to use a sledgehammer to crack a walnut, but it's bloody fun trying.

Graham Keith

I've been on a calendar, but never on time.

Marilyn Monroe

Even in today's permissive society there are four-letter words which shock most men – like cook, iron, dust and tidy.

Dave Greenhead

One mother was telling another about their hotel problems when they were on holiday.
'The food was poison – and such small portions.'

Anon

Prevalent Poetry

A wandering tribe called the Siouxs,
Wear moccasins, having no shiouxs.
   They are made of buckskin,
   With the fleshy side in,
Embroidered with beads of bright hyiouxs.

When out on the war-path the Sioux
March single-file – never by tiouxs –
   And by 'blazing' the trees
   Can return at their ease,
And their way through the forest ne'er liouxs.

All new-fashioned boats he eschiouxs,
And uses the birch-bark caniouxs,
   These are handy and light,
   And, inverted at night,
Give shelter from storms and from dyiouxs.

The principal food of the Siouxs
Is Indian maize, which they briouxs
   And hominy make,
   Or mix in a cake
And eat it with pork, as they chiouxs.

Now doesn't this spelling look cyiouxrious?
'Tis enough to make anyone fyiouxrious?
   So a word to the wise!
   Pray our language revise
With orthography not so injiouxrious.

Andrew Lang

Laugh and be merry, remember, better the world
   with a song,
Better the world with a blow in the teeth of a wrong.
Laugh, for the time is brief, a thread the length of a span
Laugh, and be proud to belong to the old proud pageant
   of man

John Masefield

Smiles and laughter have settled more disputes and saved more awkward situations than all life's logic, philosophy and economics put together.

Linton Andrews

Politicians

'A Politician is a man who approaches every question
with an open mouth.'

Oscar Wilde

– *Inspiration* –

Efficiency of a practically flawless kind may be reached naturally in the struggle for bread. But there is something beyond – a higher point, a subtle and unmistakeable touch of love and pride beyond mere skill; almost an inspiration which gives to all work that finish which is almost art – which is art.

Joseph Conrad from *The Mirror of the Sea*

Inspiration

The morning ripe with promise
a fruited tree waiting to be harvested
flourishes in the garden of mind.

What life springs from its branches
or depths of dreams rooted there?
What lies dormant, in a fog,
waiting for the light of awareness?

In these serene moments of dawn
let me explore the garden
in search of fruitful inspiration,
I am thirsty for sweet nectar.

Carolyn Brunelle

Star of Eternal Possibles and Joy

Star of eternal possibles and joy,
Vibrate the marble with your kiss!
On ancient columns and dark walls
    Fall with unearthly calls,
Bird-supple wings disturbing air!

Fall like the rain on praying hands;
Bring to the living-haunted hills
Remote perspectives and new worlds –
    Invasion of the wilds,
Illumination of nocturnal fairs.

Disturb the logic of bleak winds –
Rotations of the mind unwinding life;
And in the midnight waiting groves,
    The ever-talking graves
Crying aloud the perfect word.

Aim for the fringe, the thinnest curve
Where strength of possible despairs:
The missing but imagined arc
    For which the circle aches,
The vista waiting to be seen.

Peter Yates

It Couldn't Be Done

Somebody said that it couldn't be done,
   But he with a chuckle replied
That 'maybe it couldn't', but he would be one
   Who wouldn't say so till he'd tried.
So he buckled right in with the trace of a grin
   On his face. If he worried he hid it.
He started to sing as he tackled the thing
   That couldn't be done, and he did it.

Somebody scoffed: 'Oh, you'll never do that;
   At least no one ever has done it';
But he took off his coat and he took off his hat,
   And the first thing we knew he'd begun it.
With a lift of his chin and a bit of a grin,
   Without any doubting or quiddit,
He started to sing as he tackled the thing
   That couldn't be done, and he did it.

There are thousands to tell you it cannot
   be done,
   There are thousands to prophesy failure;
There are thousands to point out to you,
   one by one,
   The dangers that wait to assail you.
But just buckle in with a bit of a grin,

Just take off your coat and go to it;
Just start to sing as you tackle the thing
   That 'cannot be done', and you'll do it.

Edgar A. Guest

My Purpose

To awaken each morning with a smile brightening
   my face;

To greet the day with reverence for the opportunities
   it contains;

To approach my work with a clean mind;

To hold ever before me, even in the doing of little
   things, the Ultimate Purpose toward which I am
   working;

To meet men and women with laughter on my lips and
   love in my heart;

To be gentle, kind, and courteous through all the hours;

To approach the night with weariness that ever woos
   sleep, and the joy that comes from work well done –

This is how I desire to waste wisely my days.

Thomas Dekker

The only social security any able man needs is a good place
to work, a good place to worship, and a good home to love.

James J. O'Reilly

The Adventurous Life

The only life worth living is the adventurous life. Of such a life the dominant characteristic is that it is unafraid. It is unafraid of what other people think. Like Columbus, it dares not only to assert a belief but to live it in the face of contrary opinion. It does not adapt either its pace or its objectives to the pace and objectives of its neighbours. It thinks its own thoughts, it reads its own books, it develops its own hobbies, and it is governed by its own conscience. The herd may graze where it pleases or stampede where it pleases, but he who lives the adventurous life will remain unafraid when he finds himself alone.

Raymond B. Fosdick

Inspiration

It is said that hope goes with youth; but I fancy that hope is the last gift given to man, and the only gift not given to youth. For youth the end of every episode is the end of the world. But the power of hoping through everything, the knowledge that the soul survives its adventures – that great inspiration comes to the middle-aged.

G. K. Chesterton

Inspiration

As I look at people who overcome the impossible I reflect on all things that are good. I lend the warmth and compassion to those in need. As I continue through the corridors of life I search for the inspirational light that burns bright within each and every person on any given night.

John Fritz Jr.

Thomas Jefferson's Decalogue

I.   Never put off till tomorrow what you can do today.

II. Never trouble another for what you can do yourself.

III. Never spend your money before you have it.

IV. Never buy what you do not want, because it is cheap; it will be dear to you.

V.   Pride costs us more than hunger, thirst, and cold.

VI. We never repent of having eaten too little.

VII. Nothing is troublesome that we do willingly.

VIII. How much pain have cost us the evils which have never happened.

IX. Take things always by their smooth handle.

X.   When angry, count ten before you speak; if very angry, an hundred.

My Symphony

To live content with small means;

To seek elegance rather than luxury,
and refinement rather than fashion;

To he worthy, not respectable, and wealthy,
not rich;

To study hard, think quietly, talk gently,
act frankly;

To listen to stars and birds, to babes and sages,
with open heart;

To hear all cheerfully, do all bravely, await
occasions, hurry never.

In a word, to let the spiritual, unbidden and
unconscious, grow up through the common.

This is to be my symphony.

William Ellery Channing

Starlight Inspiration

Oh, stars of the night...

Burning spheres of flaming fire,

Bright, bold, glittering the heavens,

I gasp breathlessly at your beauty.

Flickering prisms of universal color

Exclaiming God's powers throughout infinity.

Artistically splashed to warmly light the
darkness.

Milky patterns of heavenly creations.
Miracles in motion for the soul's delight.
    A super-natural testimony
Of God's celestial handiwork.
Silvery masses of pure energy
Majestic immaculate constellations
Multicolored planets in perfected rotation.
    Oh, starry, starry skies...
How powerful were the hands that formed you.
Intelligence far beyond imagination
Spoke you into existence.
Loyal is He that gives you fuel to shine
Night after night without fail.
Faithfully He guards over His vast solar system
And all is beautifully balanced. Stars that shine,
    truly friends of mine...
The gift of eternity lies there beyond
A promise of burning life
A miracle for us to grasp.
His dreamy Starlight Inspiration for us all
    to share.

Linda Lara

– Love –

Love is the great instrument of nature, the bond and cement of society, the spirit and spring of the universe. Love is such an affection as cannot so properly be said to be in the soul, as the soul to be in that: it is the whole nature wrapped up into one desire.

Robert Southey

I never saw love as luck, as that gift from the gods which put everything else in place, and allowed you to succeed. No, I saw love as *reward*. One could find it only after one's virtue, or one's courage, or self-sacrifice, or generosity, or loss, has succeeded in stirring the power of creation.

Norman Mailer

Yet, Love, Mere Love, is Beautiful Indeed

Yet, love, mere love, is beautiful indeed
And worthy of acceptation. Fire is bright,
Let temple burn, or flax; an equal light
Leaps in the flame from cedar-plank or weed:
And love is fire. And when I say at need
I love thee … mark! … I love thee – in thy sight
I stand transfigured, glorified aright,
With conscience of the new rays that proceed

Out of my face toward thine. There's nothing low
In love, when love the lowest: meanest creatures
Who love God, God accepts while loving so.
And what I feel, across the inferior features
Of what I am, doth flash itself, and show
How that great work of Love enhances Nature's.

Elizabeth Barrett Browning

Love's Philosophy

The fountains mingle with the river
And the rivers with the Ocean.
The winds of Heaven mix for ever
With a sweet emotion;
Nothing in the world is single;
All things by a law divine
In one spirit meet and mingle
Why not I with thine?

See the mountains kiss high Heaven
And the waves clasp one another;
No sister-flower would be forgiven
If it disdained its brother.

Percy Bysshe Shelley

The Goal of Intellectual Man

The goal of intellectual man
Striving to do what he can
To bring down out of uncreated light
Illumination to our night

Is not possession of the fire
Annihilation of his own desire
To the source a secret soaring
And all his self outpouring

Nor is it an imageless place
Wherein there is no human face
Nor laws, nor hierarchies, nor dooms
And only the cold weight of the tomb

But it is human love, love
Concrete, specific, in a natural move
Gathering goodness, it is free
In the blood as in the mind's harmony,

It is love discoverable here
Difficult, dangerous, pure, clear,
The truth of the positive hour
Composing all of human power.

Richard Eberhart

Lovers' Lane

When day is ended and the world is wrapped in
     evening's calm

the lovers down the leafy lane go strolling arm in arm;

they dream Love's gay romantic dreams, exploring magic
     realms

until the moon comes peeping through the tangle of the
     elms...

Then homeward to the village where the lighted
     windows gleam –

enchanted in the secret rapture of a lover's dream...

What ardent hopes are harboured in the heart of man
     and maid!

the common earth is holy ground, when brave and
     unafraid,

they view from Youth's high peak of faith the years that
     are to be

and heart to heart they make their vows for all
     Eternity...

Oh, may they never lose this sense of magic and delight

that clings about them as they walk, enraptured, through
     the night...

No matter what the years may hold of pleasure or
     of pain

May life for them be one long stroll along a lovers' lane.

Patience Strong

How Do I Love Thee?
Let Me Count the Ways

How do I love thee? Let me count the ways.
I love thee to the depth and breadth and height
my soul can reach, when feeling out of sight.
For the ends of Being, an ideal Grace.
I love thee to the level of every day's
Most quiet need; by sun and candle-light.
I love thee freely, as men strive for Right;
I love thee purely, as they turn from Praise.
I love thee with the passion put to use
In my old griefs, and with my childhood's faith.
I love thee with a love I seemed to lose
With my lost saints, I love thee with the breath,
Smiles, tears, of all my life! and, if God choose,
I shall but love thee better after death.

Elizabeth Barrett Browning

On Love

To be in love demands that the lover shall divine the wishes of the beloved long before they have come into the beloved's own consciousness. He knows her better than she knows herself; and loves her more than she loves herself; so that she becomes her perfect self without her own conscious effort. *Her* conscious effort, when the love is mutual, is for him. Thus each delightfully works perfection in the other.

But this state is not ordinarily attained in nature: it is the fruit of art, of self-training. All people desire it, even the most cynical; but since it seldom occurs by chance, and nobody has published the key to its creation, the vast majority doubt even its possibility. Nevertheless it is possible, provided that the parties can learn and teach humbly. How to begin? Let the lover when he is about to see his beloved think what he should take, do, or say so as to give her a delightful surprise. At first it will probably be a surprise that is not a complete surprise: that is to say, she will have been aware of her wish, and only delighted that her lover had guessed it. Later the delightful surprise may really surprise her; and her remark will be: 'How did you know I should be pleased, since I should never have guessed it myself?' Constant efforts to anticipate the nascent wishes of the beloved while they are still unconscious are the means to conscious love.

A. R. Orage

All-Embracing Love

Love all God's creation, both the whole and every grain of sand. Love every leaf, every ray of light. Love the animals, love the plants, love each separate thing. If thou love each thing thou will perceive the mystery of God in all; and when once thou perceive this, thou wilt thenceforward grow every day to a fuller understanding of it: until thou come at last to love the whole world with a love that will then be all-embracing and universal.

Fyodor Dostoyevski

We Say I Love You

We say, 'I love you', in many ways: with Valentines and birthday presents, with smiles and tears, with poems and cups of tea; sometimes by keeping our mouths shut, other times by speaking out, even brusquely; sometimes by gentleness, by listening, by thoughtfulness, by impulsiveness. Frequently we must love by forgiving someone who has not listened for the love we tried to express to him.

Paul Tillich

Moon follows moon
before the Great Moon
flowers, Moon of the
wild, wild honey that is ours!
Long must the tree strive up
in leaf and root
Before it bear the golden-
hearted fruit,
And shall great love at
once perfected spring,
Nor grow by steps like
any other thing?

Richard le Gallienne

Love

Love is never absent from the air.
I find it there, each time
the me that blocks the view
has wandered off, somewhere;

Like many tricky friends
I knew in school,
love reaches round my back
and taps me on the shoulder
so I turn and look
away from where she stands.
But I am not so stupid
that I do not know her hands.

And when she uses them
to hide my eyes
and whispers in my ears,
'guess who?'
my smile grows so wide
that there is only smile
and nothing else, inside.

Kevan Myers

Untitled

… but a piercing emptiness
to pierce the pitcher
fills this moment now.
Peace, the snowy blossom
on the bough outside
has turned me into old leaves
opening russet gold
to redden old coals under earth
for the spring to come.
I love you
because I am; you are.

Jane Adams

You And Me

You are a tree that has grown in me.
From some small germ beginning,
seed sown on any of many
half forgotten afternoons,
your stirring plant reared suddenly to life
and quickened all my being.

Twice did I turn away and roam;
but from some remaining meristem
resurged your growth and uttered

its strange beauty through my core.
So stretch your branches through my
    limbs
and, dark within, your searching roots
twist deeper in my soil; and with
strange pleasure I feel the pain
of your increasing pressure,
nor ever more breathe nay.

Now in the cool
of these last treasured days,
far from the thrust of those
first strenuous ways,
there is no call
to be reminded that
'This single song of two
this is a wonder.'

Peter Adams

If you bring sunshine into the lives of others,
    you cannot keep the rays from yourself.

Anon

Master, what is the best way to meet the loss of someone we love?

By knowing that when we truly love, it is never lost. It is only after death that the depth of the bond is truly felt, and our loved one becomes more a part of us than was possible in life.

Are we only able to feel this toward those whom we have known and loved a long time?

Sometimes a stranger, known to us for moments, can spark our souls to kinship for eternity.

How can strangers take on such importance to our souls?

Because our soul does not keep time, it merely records growth.

Love cannot measure itself until the hour of parting. Trust comes from within you. Is not to trust, to rely on someone of whom you know nothing? With each ending comes a new beginning.

> I seek not to know all the answers,
> but to understand the questions.

Oriental Tradition

– *Magic* –

Magic of the Deep

When the breath of twilight blows to flame the
misty skies,

All its vaporous sapphire, violet glow and silver gleam,

With their magic flood me through the gateway of
the eyes;

I am one with the twilight's dream.

George W. Russell ('AE')
From *By the Margin of the Great Deep.*

Universal Magic

It's the song of the world.
The tune of everyone's life.
It's the caressing wind.
The ever present nature spills
magic into the air and infuses
it into the bones of every being
on the planet. It gives a certain
strength to those in need of it.
Also this magic fills the heart of
the weak and makes them strong.
This universal magic has begun its work

Rae Taylor

Magic

I ask myself in the dead of night
What is this magic what is this might
Is it the curse of an old wizened maid
With a twisted wand from hazel made
Or is it a potion from some secret blend
To alter another or their life just to end
Then maybe it's a spell or dire incantation
That weaves a web with no protection
Perhaps at some level this may, with strain
Effect a change, but then again
It's not what I would call magic

Magic for me is the first ray of dawn
It's a clump of daffodils in a country lawn
A child's first breath or a stormy sea
These hold so much more magic for me
A spider's web hung with dew
The tiniest egg that to human grew
But far away more magical than this
Was the moment our lips first touched in a kiss
Then my heart beat so fast I was happy to die
And my soul sang a song as it learned how to fly
And that's what I would call magic

Shaun William Hayes

In Pleasant Places

By 'magic' I don't mean abracadabra and fairy godmothers with wishes, nor do I mean witches and spells and funny goings on at seances.

I mean the heightened quality of certain, often quite small, experiences lit by unexplained excitement, powerful with innocence. It can come from looking hard at a shell, arriving at an unexpected view of the sea, hearing a bar of music.

> To see a World in a Grain of Sand,
>
> And a Heaven in a Wild Flower,
>
> Hold Infinity in the palm of your hand,
>
> And Eternity in an hour.

Some of my contemporaries don't agree with me that this kind of magic is far more potent in middle age than when one was new. It is so for me because now I bring more to each experience, and 'magic' is very nourishing.

Places induce it. East Anglia. The bush in Australia. I get it particularly in a certain small valley in Cumberland. The first time I went there, having chosen a place to stay from an unillustrated guide-book with just an inch of unexaggerated prose, we drove across a high bare pass and as we came near it I knew – this is it! I said it out loud, too. It was recognition, and I get it unfailingly every time I go back there. (I get it whenever I make a new discovery of *anything*.) I don't think I knew what people meant when they said a place was their spiritual home. But I do now.

Joyce Grenfell

Magic!

The heart is the magician.

Poet's words swirl in an endless void running to
    catch an eternal wind.

Our human spirit magically emerges from the
    magician's hat;

the soul finding its equal in a sea of colour.

Music,

art,

sound,

life,

paint,

emerges from the void of the human heart.

Time ceases to exist.

Only the artist sees the heartbeat in footsteps
    that cross London streets.

Only the musician hears the melody in the
    human voice.

Laughter, conversation that ebbs and flows like
    music in morning rush-hour cafes echoes a
    note contributing to a grander symphony.

Buildings conceived by artists are Picasso's
    dream.

In London,

life has its own energy.

The artist paints an abstraction of the Thames as
    it collides with the sun.

Modernity of steel and glass plays hop-skotch

with cobblestone streets and Shakespeare's
    laughter echoes through time.

In London,

water learns how to breathe within a
    composition of sound.

And love rushes between windows trying to
    capture a whisper.

Judith Vriesema

Oh, what a catastrophe for man when he cut himself off
from the rhythm of the year, from his unison with the sun
and the earth. Oh, what a catastrophe, what a maiming of
love when it was a personal, merely personal feeling, taken
away from the rising and the setting of the sun, and cut off
from the magic connection of the solstice and the equinox!

D. H. Lawrence

But these young scholars, who invade our hills,
Bold as the engineer who fells the wood,
And travelling often in the cut he makes,
Love not the *flower* they pluck, and know it not
And all their botany is Latin names.
The old men studied magic in the flowers.

Ralph Waldo Emerson

Magic Spectacles

If only we could buy some magic spectacles to wear

through which the world would seem to be a heaven
good and fair

No sordid slums, no captive things, no horses with
'their' loads

no idle folks, no empty hands, no blood upon the roads

no mad destruction of God's gifts midst lack and poverty

no arsenals, no hunger-marchers and no tyranny

But healthy people, good clean towns and lasting peace
on earth

and life devoted to high aims and things of greatest worth.

Yet this would be illusion, we must face the facts and see

without our magic spectacles the grim Reality;

perhaps we must have ugliness that beauty might be prized

perhaps the evil must exist that Good be recognised ...

There is the right way and the wrong

the human and divine

God's work is perfect, it is man who spoils the 'great'
design.

Patience Strong

Why not walk in the aura of magic that gives to the small
things of life their uniqueness and importance? Why not
befriend a toad today?

Germaine Greer

There is no real teacher who in practise does not believe in the existence of the soul, or in a magic that acts on it through speech.

Allan Bloom

Cats exercise ... a magic influence upon highly developed men of intellect. This is why these long-tailed Graces of the animal kingdom, these adorable, scintillating electric batteries have been the favorite animal of a Mohammed, Cardinal Richlieu, Crebillon, Rousseau, Wieland.

Leopold von Sacher-Masoch

Magic And Genius

Whatever you can do, or dream you can do, begin it.
Boldness has power, magic and genius in it.

Johann Wolfgang von Goethe

Wizardry

There's many a proud wizard in Araby and Egypt
   Can read the silver writing of the stars as they rùn;
And many a dark gypsy, with a pheasant in his
   knapsack,
   Has gathered more by moonshine than wiser men
  have won;

But *I* know a Wizardry
   Can take a buried acorn
And whisper forests out of it, to tower against the sun.

There's many a magician in Baghdad and Benares
   Can read you – for a penny – what your future
     is to be;
And a flock of crazy prophets that by staring at a crystal
   Can fill it with more fancies than there's herring in
     the sea;

But *I* know a Wizardry
   Can break a freckled egg-shell
And shake a throstle out of it, in every hawthorn-tree.

There's many a crafty alchemist in Mecca and Jerusalem;
   And Michael Scott and Merlin were reckoned
     very wise;

But *I* know a Wizardry
   Can take a wisp of sun fire
And round it to a planet and roll it through the skies,
   With cities, and sea-ports, and little shining windows,
And hedgerows and gardens, and loving human eyes …

Alfred Noyes

144

MAGIC

Three Words from a Magic Bird

By cunning and a carefully set trap, a man once caught a bird. To his surprise, when he was about to kill and eat it, the bird spoke to him.

'My dear sir', it said, 'you've eaten sheep and even oxen in your time, and have risen from the table still hungry, so it's hardly likely that you'll get any satisfaction out of what little flesh is on my bones. However, if you will set me free I will be able to give you three wise sayings which will be of great value to you. What do you say?'

The astonished man agreed.

'Very well, then,' said the bird. 'Listen carefully. The first saying I will give you as soon as you open your hand. The second I will give you from your own rooftop, and the third from that tree over there. If you heed what I say you will reap a fortune. So, now, if you're ready...?'

The man opened his hand.

'Thank you', said the bird. 'Now, this is the first saying: If what you hear is obvious nonsense, don't believe it, whoever tells it to you.'

Having said this, the bird quickly flew up to the roof. 'Here is the second saying', it cried. 'Don't grieve over what is past, forget it.' Then the bird continued: 'I have to tell you now that I have swallowed a precious pearl, fully ten dirams in weight, a pearl that would have brought wealth and prosperity to you and your descendants for generations to come. But, by releasing me, you have lost it!'

At this the man cried aloud, wailing piteously, tearing his clothes in anguish and regret.

'Come, come,' the bird called down. 'What is the point of my giving you these wise sayings if you don't heed them? Was not my second saying, just now, that you should not regret what is past? Do stop this noise, therefore. And you paid as little heed to my first saying as you did to the second.'

'How so?' sobbed the man.

'Did I not tell you not to believe obvious nonsense?

'I myself weigh only a couple of dirams. You know that, for you have held me in your hand. How then could I have, concealed within me, a pearl weighing ten dirams?'

'O, of course, of course', cried the relieved man. 'So now, O wise bird, give me the third saying.'

The bird flew to the tree.

'Knowing what use you have made of my first two sayings,' said the bird, 'I have decided that my third will also be wasted on you. And so, farewell.'

And away it flew.

Idries Shah

– *Miracles* –

Miracles

I dreamt I saw a huge grey boat in silence steaming
Down a canal; it drew the dizzy landscape after;
The solemn world was sucked along with it –
    a streaming
Land-slide of loveliness. O, but I rocked with laughter,
Staring, and clinging to my tree-top. For a lake
Of gleaming peace swept on behind. (I mustn't wake.)

And then great clouds gathered and burst in spumes
    of green
That plunged into the water, and the sun came out
On glittering islands thronged with orchards scarlet-
    bloomed;
And rosy-plumed flamingoes flashed across the scene …
O, but the beauty of their freedom made me shout …
And when I woke I wondered where on earth I'd been.

Siegfried Sassoon

Miracles are like jokes. They relieve our tension suddenly
by setting us free from the chain of cause and effect.

Gerald Branan

PEACE *of* MIND

Miracles

To me, every hour of the light and dark is a miracle,

Every cubic inch of space is a miracle,

Every square yard of the surface of the earth is spread
    with the same,

Every foot of the interior swarms with the same;

Every spear of grass – the frames, limbs, organs, of men
    and women, and all that concerns them,

All these to me are unspeakably perfect miracles.

To me the sea is a continual miracle;

The fishes that swim – the rocks – the motion of the
    waves – the ships, with men in them,

What stranger miracles are there?

Walt Whitman

Miracles

Each time that I switch on the light

A Miracle it seems to me

That I should rediscover sight

And banish dark so utterly.

One moment I am bleakly blind,

The next – exultant life I find.

Below the sable of the sky

My eyelids double darkness make.

Sleep is divine, yet oh how I
Am glad with wonder to awake!
To welcome, glimmery and wan
The mighty Miracle of Dawn.

For I've mad moments when I seem,
With all the marvel of a child,
To dwell within a world of dream,
To sober fact unreconciled.
Each simple act has struck me thus –
Incredibly miraculous.

When everything I see and do
So magical can seem to me,
How vain it is to seek the True,
The riddle of Reality …
So let me with joy lyrical
Proclaim all Life a Miracle!

Robert W. Service

Miracles

Why, who makes much of a miracle?
As to me I know of nothing else but miracles
Whether I tread the moonlit path,
Or hear the first cry uttered by a new-born baby,

Or ponder over the journey from infancy to death,

Or see the thirsty earth being satiated by the cool
    showers of rain,

Or listen to the mellifluous tunes pouring forth from
    a flute,

Or being awakened byt he cockadoodling of a cock
    at dawn,

Or see the beautiful colours of the rainbow adorning
    the sky,

Or feel the power of the wind shaking up the
    droopy leaves,

Or marvel when two strangers fall in love,

Or wonder at God's presence when He answers
    my prayers.

Every muscle in me is a miracle!

Every drop of blood in me is a miracle!

Every strand of hair of mine is a miracle!

A miracle is happening here and now,

If only you could see,

Every creation is a miracle,

Like this world, these words and I.

Francisca Simon

The student of Nature wonders the more and is astonished the less, the more conversant he becomes with her operations; but of all the perennial miracles she offers to his inspection, perhaps the most worthy of admiration is the development of a plant or of an animal from its embryo.

Thomas Henry Huxley

Miracle

Do not pray for easy lives; pray to be stronger men. Do not pray for tasks equal to your powers; pray for powers equal to your tasks. Then the doing of your work shall be no miracle, but you shall be a miracle. Every day you shall wonder at yourself, at the richness of life which has come to you by the grace of God.

Phillips Brooks

How many a man has dated a new era in his life from the reading of a book! The book exists for us, perchance, that will explain our miracles and reveal new ones. The at present unutterable things we may find somewhere uttered.

Henry David Thoreau

A miracle, my friend, is an event which creates faith. That is the purpose and nature of miracles. They may seem very wonderful to the people who witness them, and very simple to those who perform them. That does not matter: if they confirm or create faith they are true miracles.

George Bernard Shaw

– *Money* –

Never ask of money spent
Where the spender thinks it went.
Nobody was ever meant
To remember or invent
What he did with every cent.

Robert Frost

There's more lying about money than about any other one thing in the world. Money isn't half the curse it's often painted – nor half the blessing. It all depends on who owns it.

B. C. Forbes

Money is like an arm or a leg – use it or lose it.

Henry Ford

There'll be no pockets in your shroud.

James T. Hill

People never discuss their salaries publicly, or their income, or their patrimony. People make a successful effort never to discuss money in front of friends or relatives, because money in our society is the ultimate reality and to discuss it is to reveal oneself.

Harry Golden

Here's to our town – a place where people spend money they haven't earned to buy things they don't need to impress people they don't like.

Lewis C. Henry

What I know about money, I learned the hard way – by having had it.

Margaret Halsey

Money is like honey: a little of it is sweet, but a
superabundance cloys.

B. C. Forbes

When a man says money can do anything,
that settles it; he hasn't any.

E. W. Howe

M stands fer money, root of evil an' vice,
However, nothin' succeeds like havin' th' price.

Frank McKinney

Nobody works as hard for his money
as the man who marries it.

Frank McKinney

You can't take it with you.

Moss Hart

Never spend your money before you have it.

Thomas Jefferson

Floral Symphony

The rose composed a symphony –
With love poured out its heart.
The other flowers in great delight
Each clamoured for a part.

The poppy played the piccolo,
The foxglove chose the flute,
The violet, the violin.
While the lupin strummed the lute.

The daisy played the double bass,
The buttercup, bassoon.
The chrysanthemum crashed the cymbals!!!
And fell into a swoon...

The sunflower almost strained itself
Playing the saxophone...

The cornflower tried the clarinet –
But gave up with a groan.

The dahlia tried to play the drum
But went quite off its head,

So they took away the drum –
And made it play the harp instead!

The peony on piano
A virtuoso proved,
The orchid on the oboe
Left everybody moved.

The carnation as conductor
Was a most impressive sight
And rehearsed the flowers for ages
To make sure they got it right.

The symphony was a great success,
Everyone called for more.
No garden it seemed had ever been
So much in tune before!

Paul Johnson

When music sounds, gone is the earth I know,
And all her lovely things even lovelier grow;
Her flowers in vision flame, her forest trees
Lift burdened branches, stilled with ecstasies.

When music sounds, out of the water rise
Naiads whose beauty dims my waking eyes,

Rapt in strange dreams burns each
    enchanted face,
With solemn echoing stirs their dwelling-place.

When music sounds, all that I was I am
Ere to this haunt of brooding dust I came;
And from Time's woods break into distant song
The swift-winged hours, as I hasten along.

Walter de la Mare

Everyone Sang

Everyone suddenly burst out singing;
And I was filled with such delight
As prisoned birds must find in freedom
Winging wildly across the white
Orchards and dark green fields;
    on – on – and out of sight.
Everyone's voice was suddenly lifted;
And beauty came like the setting sun:
My heart was shaken with tears; and horror
Drifted away … O but Everyone
Was a bird; and the song was wordless;
    the singing will never be done.

Seigfried Sassoon

Unfinished Journey

Music is given us with our existence. An infant cries, or crows or talks with his own voice and goes one step beyond to sing. Above other arts, music can be possessed without knowledge; being an expression largely of the subconscious, it has its direct routes from whatever is in our guts, minds and spirits, without need of a detour through the classroom. That direct route I knew, thank God. I learned to love music before I learned to say so; I was given the raw material when I could scarcely read or write; I early felt the wonder of taking up a violin and making it speak, communicate with others, express the thoughts and feelings of great composers. No doubt I had great aptitude which enabled me to excel my teachers in specific performances, but this phenomenon is generally accounted more mysterious than it is. Violin in hand, a talented youngster with music in his heart, an inspiring master, and the capacity to play by 'feel' and imitation can hurdle obstacles apparently insuperable to the adult mind, which would erect barriers of qualification to be surmounted before one wins the right to self-expression.

Yehudi Menuhin

The song that we hear with our ears is only the song
that is sung in our hearts.

Ouida

Cello Concert At St Martin's

YES! The boy child came
with his cello to the church,
laid over his heart four strings,
lifted his bow, let love be a
sacred Temple:

six whole suites of Bach
I heard the Angel
through him, play.

Lord of the Dance!
Soundboard tenor clef,
I sing in the ground,
I am the Way, the Lord of the Dance,
    said he;
a vortex into my body pegged.

The thief in the night
broke into my soul at dawn.

I am the Lord of the Dance, said he,
spread over the heavens his flame.
The Angel, he said, destroys
with beating wing, my name –
and I weep to give up

and I laugh to be *Templi omnium*
    hominum pacis abbas.

In the Temple of Peace for All,
nothing divides the human heart.
Broken pieces fall into peace
where Temple dancer turns –
the firestick twirling, burns
the dross like rising dhoop –
this savour to the Lord of the Dance
is pleasing.

Then I
am the Lord of the Dance, said he,
four arms Four Worlds a-dancing:
    toe pegged into me.

Again he laid across his heart
    four strings
and spike in floorboard knot,
raised bow, closed eyes,
gave Bach's
psalms in the breaking tide
in the church,
no wars nor waves between.

I am upon four strings
and in four worlds
the Lord of the Dance, said he.
And let love be
as you will!

Jane Adams

An Die Musik

O lovely art, in how many grey hours
When the wild round of life ensnared me
Have you kindled my heart to warm love
And carried me into a better world.

Often has a sigh, flowing from my harp,
A sweet and holy harmony from you,
Unlocked for me the heaven of better times.
O lovely art, I thank you for it.

Franz Schubert

Music creates order out of chaos; for rhythm imposes
unanimity upon the divergent, melody imposes continuity
upon the disjointed, and harmony imposes compatibility
upon the incongruous.

Yehudi Menuhin

The basic difference between classical music and jazz is that in the former the music is always greater than its performance – whereas the way jazz is performed is always more important than what is being played.

André Previn

Seated one day at the organ,
I was weary and ill at ease,
And my fingers wandered idly
Over the noisy keys.
But I struck one chord of music,
Like the sound of a great Amen.

Adelaide Anne Procter

Music exalts each joy, allays each grief,
Expels diseases, softens every pain,
Subdues the rage of poison and the plague.

John Armstrong, M.D.

To the music of Rimsky-Korsakoff
I could never take my corset off
And where are the sailors who would pay
To see me strip to Massenet?

Gypsy Rose Lee

What humiliation when someone stood next to me and heard a flute in the distance and I heard nothing, or when someone heard the shepherd boy singing and again I heard nothing. Such misfortunes brought me to the edge of despair, and I might have brought an end to my life – only my art held me back. Oh, it seemed impossible to me to quit this world until I had produced everything I felt I could produce.

Ludwig van Beethoven

Applause is a receipt, not a bill.

Artur Schnabel

The First Musician

The ancient and valiant Wainamoinen washed his thumbs; he purified his fingers; he seated himself by the sea upon the Stone of Joy, upon the Hillock of Silver, even at the summit of the Hill of Gold; and he took the instrument within his hands and lifted up his voice, saying: 'Let him that hath never heard the strong joy of runes, the sweet sound of instruments, the sound of music, come hither and hear.'

And the ancient Wainamoinen began to sing. Limpid his voice as the voice of running water, deep and clear, mighty and beautiful …

All the living creatures of the forest, all the living creatures of the air, drew nigh unto the rune-singer, gathered themselves about the mighty chanter, that they might hear the suavity of his voice, that they might taste the sweetness of his song ... All the heroes wept; the hardest of hearts were softened ... The youths wept; the old men wept; the virgins wept; the little infants wept; even Wainamoinen also felt the source of his own tears rising to overflow....

They streamed upon his cheeks, and from his cheeks they fell upon his knees, and from his knees they dropped upon his feet, and from his feet they rolled into the dust. And his tear-drops passed through his six garments of wool, his six girdles of gold, his seven robes of blue, his eight tunics all thickly woven.

And the tears of Wainamoinen flowed as a river, and became a river, and poured themselves to the shores of the sea, and precipitated themselves from the shores into the deeps of the abyss into the region of black sands.

There did they blossom; there were they transformed into pearls, – pearls destined for the crowns of Kings, for the eternal joy of noblest heroes.

From *The Kalevala* – Finnish Tradition

If nobody wants to go to your concert,
nothing will stop them.

Isaac Stern

– *Mystery* –

The most beautiful experience we can have is the mysterious. It is the fundamental emotion which stands at the cradle of true art and true science.

Albert Einstein

The world of the living contains enough marvels and mysteries as it is; marvels and mysteries acting upon our emotions and intelligence in ways so inexplicable that it would almost justify the conception of life as an enchanted state.

Joseph Conrad

Each time dawn appears, the mystery
is there in its entirety.

René Daumal

Use and want make all life a commonplace thing. Our ordinary minds demand an ordinary world and feel at ease only when they have explained and taken for granted the mysteries among which we have been given so short a license to breathe.

Llewelyn Powys

As I make my slow pilgrimage through the world, a certain sense of beautiful mystery seems to gather and grow.

A. C. Benson

India! What mysteries does the very mention of its name not bring to mind?

Robert Benchley

Mystery of the Sea

Those who in childhood have had solitary communing with the sea know the sea's prophecy. They know that there is a deeper sympathy between the sea and the soul of man than other people dream of. They know that the water seems nearer akin than the land to the spiritual world, inasmuch as it is one and individual, and has motion, and answers to the mysterious call of the winds, and is the writing tablet of the moon and stars.

Theodore Watts-Duncan
from Aylwin the Renascence of Wonder

The mysterious is always attractive.
People will always follow a veil.

Bede Jarrett

Midas and his Golden Touch

The story of a man who fulfilled a prophecy and whose dream came true ... but then became a dreadful curse.

Before King Midas was even a king of Phrygia – in fact, when he was still a little baby – he was left lying in the garden of his parents' palace. When it was time for his nursemaid to bring him out of the sun and into the cool of the palace, she let out a yelp of surprise.

There was a row of ants crawling up the baby prince and each one was holding a golden grain of wheat. In turn, each ant popped a golden grain into the baby's mouth, then made its way back down his body.

The nursemaid snatched up the young Midas, frantically brushed the remaining ants off him, and ran indoors to tell his parents what had happened. Rather than being upset as she'd expected, they were delighted at what she told them.

'This is a good omen!' said Midas' father. 'I'm sure of it.'

'We must go to the soothsayers to find out what it means,' his mother agreed.

The soothsayers, who could see into the future, agreed with Midas' father. This was indeed a good sign. Golden wheat meant that real gold was to come. One day, Midas would be a very rich man.

When Midas was old enough to understand, his parents told him of his future good fortune, but he soon forgot about it ... Until one day, Dionysus, the god of wine, offered to grant him a wish.

Gods didn't usually grant humans wishes, but Midas had found Dionysus' friend, Silenus, in his garden. He'd been left behind after one of the god's fantastic parties. Midas made sure that Silenus got back to Dionysus safely, which was why Midas was being offered a wish.

The king thought long and hard about what he wanted …

Suddenly, he remembered the omen of the golden grains of wheat. 'Let everything I touch turn to gold!' he said, with greedy excitement.

'Are you sure that's what you want?' grinned Dionysus, taking a gulp of wine and smacking his lips together with delight.

'Yes!' cried Midas, without a second thought.

'Then it is granted,' said Dionysus. 'Don't say I didn't warn you.'

Midas bent down and picked up a twig. The moment his fingertips touched the wood, it turned to solid gold. Then he tried a leaf, a clump of grass … an apple. Now he was enjoying himself! Hurrying back to his palace, he touched each marble column and they too turned to gold.

Midas sat down at the dinner table for a celebration feast, but it soon turned into a famine. When he reached out and touched a piece of bread, it turned to gold and he couldn't bite into it. When the wine in his golden goblet reached his lips, it too turned to solid gold and couldn't be drunk.

Hungry and thirsty, Midas rose to his feet and paced up and down the marble floor in his golden sandals. Just then, his young daughter ran into the room.

'Hullo, Daddy,' she beamed and, before he could stop her,

she threw her arms around him. The minute she touched her father the king, she turned into a solid gold statue.

Midas hurried, weeping, to find Dionysus. 'Please release me from this curse,' he begged. 'My greed got the better of me!'

'Very well,' said the god of wine, with a chuckle. 'There is a way to undo this magic,' and he told the king what he had to do.

Following these instructions, Midas hurried to the source of the river Pactolus – the place where the water springs from the ground near Mount Tmolus – and washed himself.

Two things happened instantly: he was freed from the curse of his golden touch, and the sands on the bed of the river Pactolus turned a beautiful gold, which is why they are that colour to this very day.

Greek myth

Rama and Sita

Alone in a clearing of Panchavati, Sita paced restlessly, concern for her husband and his brother growing ever greater as the moments passed. And then she was startled by a movement in the trees. Into the clearing came a wandering yogi, and Sita smiled her welcome. She would not be alone after all.

She offered the yogi food and water, and told him her identity. She kindly asked for information in return and was startled when he called himself Ravana, and asked her to renounce Rama and become his wife. Ravana gazed at the lovely Sita and a deep jealousy and anger filled his soul. He determined to have her and he cared little now for his revenge of Rama.

Now Sita was enraged by the slight afforded her husband, the great Rama, by this insolent Ravana and she lashed out at him:

'I am the servant of Rama alone, lion among men, immovable as any mountain, as vast as the great ocean, radiant as Indra. Would you draw the teeth from a lion's mouth? Or swim in the sea with a heavy stone about your neck? You are as likely to seek the sun or moon as you are me, for Rama is little like thee – he is as different as is the lion from the jackal, the elephant from the cat, the ocean from the tiny stream and gold from silver.' She stopped, fear causing her to tremble.

Ravana roared into the empty clearing, and taking his own shape once again, grabbed the lovely Sita by the hair and made to rise into the air with her. His cry woke the great vulture Jatayu, who had been sleeping in a nearby tree. He rose in outrage and warned the evil spirit of the wrath of Rama, who would certainly let no spirit live who had harmed his most prized possession. But Ravana sprang upon the poor great bird and after a heroic battle, cut away his wings, so that he fell down near death.

Ravana swept Sita into his carriage and rose into the sky. As she left the clearing, Sita cried out to the flowers, and the forest, begging them to pass on her fate to Rama and Lakshman upon their return. And then she cast down her veil and her jewels as a token for her husband.

Ravana returned her to his palace and begged her to become his wife. Her face crumpled in bitter pain and she refused to speak. And as he persisted, she turned to him then and prophesied his certain death at the hands of Rama. And she spoke no more.

Rama returned from the chase of the golden deer with an overwhelming sense of trepidation, and as he met with his brother, far from the clearing, his fears were confirmed. Rama and Lakshman raced towards the hermitage, but Sita had gone. There they found the weapons which had cut down the brave Jatayu, and the dying bird, who raised himself just enough to recount the events of the previous hours. And then, released of his burden, the soul of the great Jatayu rose above the clearing, leaving his body to sag to the ground below.

And so it was that Rama set out with Lakshman to search for Sita, travelling across the country but hearing little news and having no idea where Ravana kept his palace. He met with Sugriva, a king who had been robbed of his wife and his kingdom by his cruel brother Vali, and with the help of Hanuman, chief of the monkeys they continued their search.

Sugriva and Rama formed an alliance and it was agreed that Sugriva would be restored to his throne with the help of Rama. In return Sugriva would put at his disposal the monkey host, to find the poor Sita, already four months lost.

Rama's signet ring was put in Hanuman's possession, to show to Sita as a sign when he found her, but the monkey chief returned with his host, ashamed and saddened that they had been unable to find the beautiful princess. But then, as hope began to fade, there was news. On the coasts of the sea, where the monkeys sat deep in dejection, was a cave in which an old and very wise vulture made his home. He was Sampati, and he was brother to Jatayu. When he heard of his brother's fate he offered to the host his gift of foresight. Ravana, he announced, was with Sita in Lanka.

A brave and noble monkey, Jambavan, chose Hanuman for the task of retrieving Sita, and Hanuman swelled with pride at the prospect of his task. He sprang easily across the thousands of leagues, and across the sea – carelessly knocking down any foe who stood in his path. And so it was that he arrived on the walls of Lanka, and made his way towards the palace. The moon sat high in the sky, and the occupants of the golden city went about their nightly activities.

Making himself invisible, he entered the private apartments of Ravana, who lay sleeping with his many wives around him. But there was no sign of Sita. Hanuman roamed the city, increasingly anxious for the safety of Rama's wife, but she was not to be found. A deep desolation overtook him and he realized the enormity of his task. If he was unable to find the beautiful Sita then Lakshman and Rama would surely die of grief. And Bharata and Satrughna would die too. And the shame that would be brought on Sugriva, and the monkey host – it was too great to contemplate. Hanuman gritted his teeth, and monkey fashion swung over the palace walls and into the wood.

The wood was cool and shining with gold and gems. In its midst was a marble palace, guarded by the ugliest of rakshasis. In the palace lay the form of a woman, scantily clad in rags and thinner than any living woman.

Hanuman watched as Ravana raised himself and approached the woman, who must surely be Sita. And he watched as the woman scorned him, and ignored his advances. The glitter in her eye betrayed her identity and Hanuman leapt up and down with glee. As Ravana left, the movement of the monkey caught Sita's eye and she looked at him with distrust. Probably Ravana in disguise, she thought tiredly, used to his tricks. But Hanuman whispered to her, and spoke reams of prayers for Rama, extolling his virtues. Sita was bemused and intrigued. She leant forward to hear more. Hanuman leapt down and spoke to Sita of Rama, presenting her with his ring as a token of his continual concern for his dear wife. Sita knew then that Hanuman was friend, not foe, and she poured out stories of Rama, begging Hanuman to return at once to Rama in order that she could be rescued.

Hanuman took with him a jewel from her hair, and departed. His high spirits caused him to frolic on the way, and he could not resist destroying a few of the trees around the palace. His activities drew attention, and he fought with the rakshasas who leapt up to meet him. He wounded or slayed all who approached him until at last he was caught by the enraged Ravana, who promised him instant death.

What could be worse for a monkey, he pronounced, than having his tail set on fire? And so it was ordered that Hanuman's tail should be set alight, in order that he should burn to certain death. Now Sita still had powers of her own, and she prayed then, in Rama's name, that the fire should not burn Hanuman, but rage on at the end of his tail, leaving him unscathed. And so it was that Hanuman was able to leap away across Lanka, touching his tail here and there, in order to burn most of that glittering city to the ground. And then, dousing his tail in the wide, curving ocean, he flew across the sea to Rama.

Rama greeted Hanuman which caused the monkey to squirm with delight. He recounted all that had happened in the forest of Lanka, and he told what he had done with his burning tail. The monkey host leapt and cheered for Hanuman for he had brought them great glory with his bravery, and his craftiness.

Sugriva issued orders that all the monkey host should march to the south, in order to lay siege to Lanka. They reached the shores of the sea at Mahendra, and there they made camp. Rama joined them, and the plan to release Sita was formed.

Indian myth

The Voice, The Flood, And The Turtle

Once there was a chief whose wife, to the fear and wonder of the people, gave birth to four little monsters. The elders said: 'These strange children will bring great misfortune. It would be better to kill them right now, for the sake of the tribe.'

'No way will we kill them,' said their mother. 'These children will turn out all right, by and by.'

But they didn't turn out all right. The small monsters grew fast, much faster than ordinary children, and became very big.

They had four legs and arms each. They hurt other children; they upset tipis; they tore up buffalo robes; they befouled people's food.

A wise man, who could see things in his mind which had not yet happened, said: 'Kill these strange bad things before they kill you.'

But their mother said: 'Never. They'll be fine young men some day.'

They never became fine young men; instead they started killing and eating people. At that point all the men in the village rushed at them to do away with them, but by then it was too late. The monsters had become too big and too powerful to be killed.

They grew taller and taller. One day they went into the middle of the camp and stood back to back, one facing east, one facing south, one facing west, and one facing north. Their backs grew together, and they became one.

As they grew higher and higher, most people took refuge near the monsters' feet, where the huge creatures could not bend down to catch them. But people who strayed farther off were seized by mile-long arms, killed, and eaten. The four monsters, now grown together, rose up to the clouds, and their heads touched the sky.

Then the man who could see into the future heard a voice telling him to set up a hollow reed and plant it in the ground. The man did, and the reed grew bigger and bigger very fast. In no time it rose to touch the sky. The man heard the voice again, saying: 'I will make a great flood. When the signs of bad things coming appear, you and your wife climb up inside this hollow cane. Be naked as you were born, and take with you a pair of all the good animals in order to save them.'

The man asked: 'What sign will you be sending?'

'When all the birds in the world – birds of the woods, the sea, the deserts, and the high mountains – form up into a cloud flying from north to south, that will be the sign. Watch for the cloud of birds.'

One day the man looked up and saw a big cloud made up of birds traveling from north to south. At once he and his wife moved up into the hollow reed, taking with them all the animals they wished to save.

Then it began to rain and did not stop. Waters covered the earth and kept rising until only the top of the hollow cane and the heads of the monsters were left above the surface. Inside the hollow reed, the man and his wife heard the voice again: 'Now I shall send Turtle to destroy the monsters.'

The monsters' heads were saying to each other: 'Brothers, I'm getting tired. My legs are weakening. I can't keep standing much longer.'

The floods swirled around them with strong currents that almost swept them away. Then the Great Turtle began digging down underneath the monsters' feet. It uprooted them, and they could not keep their footing but broke apart and toppled over. They fell down into the waters, one sinking toward the north, one toward the east, one toward the south, and one toward the west. Thus the four directions came into being.

After the monsters had drowned, the waters subsided. First the mountaintops reappeared, then the rest of the land.

Next came hard-blowing winds that dried the earth. The man climbed down to the bottom of the hollow reed and opened the hole at its foot. He looked out. He stuck out his hand and felt around. He said to his wife: 'Come out. Everything is dry.'

So they emerged, followed by all the animals. They left the reed, which collapsed and disappeared. But when they stepped out on the earth, it was bare; nothing was growing.

The wife said: 'Husband, there's nothing here and we are naked. How shall we live?'

The man said: 'Go to sleep.' They lay down and slept, and when they woke the next morning, all kinds of herbs had sprung up around them.

The second night while they slept, trees and bushes grew. Now there was firewood to keep them warm, and all kinds of woods for making bows and arrows.

During the third night green grass covered the earth, and animals appeared to graze on it.

The man and his wife went to sleep a fourth time and woke up inside a grass hut. They stepped out and found a stalk of corn. Then they heard the voice say: 'This will be your holy food.' It told the woman how to plant and harvest the corn and ended with: 'Now you have everything you need. Now you can live. Now you will have children and form a new generation. If you, woman, should plant corn, and something other than corn comes up, then know that the world will come to its end.'

After that, they never heard the voice again.

[Caddo] — Retold from various sources.
Native American Tradition

– *Nature* –

You Hear Nature's Voice

You hear Nature's voice in the river that ever flows on
 towards the sea

A voice destined to live forever that has lived for untold
 centuries

From the foothills of the high country it babbles
 downhill night and day

By groves and by ditches and hedgerows to saltwater it
 winds it's way.

You hear Nature's voice in her birdsong their music
 carrying in the breeze

The sounds that the freshening winds make rustling in
 the leaves of the trees

Some of the happier sounds of Nature though to Nature
 there's another side

When Nature she shouts out her anger all others from
 her seek a safe place to hide.

When Nature she grows very angry the fear of the World
 is in her cry

She shakes the Earth flattens great buildings she roars
 and her lightning flashes in the sky

She crackles when her forests burn leaving blackness
 and smoke everywhere

With the power of Nature in a fury none other can hope
    to compare.

You hear Nature's voice in all Seasons Winter, Spring
    and Summer and Fall

And you hear Nature's voice in the night-time when her
    nocturnal creatures do call

Nature's voice will live on forever 'tis something not
    destined to die

As Nature herself does not have a time span as such are
    for mortals such as I.

Francis Duggan

All nature has a feeling

All nature has a feeling: woods, fields, brooks
Are life eternal: and in silence they
Speak happiness beyond the reach of books;
There's nothing mortal in them; their decay
Is the green life of change; to pass away
And come again in blooms revivified.
Its birth was heaven, eternal in its stay,
And with the sun and moon shall still abide
Beneath their day and night and heaven wide.

John Clare

From the Pageant of Summer

Up in the corner a fragment of white fur and marks of scratching show where a doe has been preparing for a litter. Some well-trodden runs lead from mound to mound; they are sandy near the hedge where the particles have been carried out adhering to the rabbits' feet and fur. A crow rises lazily from the upper end of the field, and perches in the chestnut. His presence, too, was unsuspected. He is there by far too frequently. At this season the crows are always in the mowing-grass, searching about, stalking in winding tracks from furrow to furrow, picking up an egg here and a foolish fledgling that has wandered from the mound yonder. Very likely there may be a moorhen or two slipping about under cover of the long grass; thus hidden, they can leave the shelter of the flags and wander a distance from the brook. So that beneath the surface of the grass and under the screen of the leaves there are ten times more birds than are seen.

Richard Jefferies

Seeking Beauty

Cold winds can never freeze, nor thunder sour
The cup of cheer that Beauty draws for me
Out of those Azure heavens and this green earth
I drink and drink, and thirst the more I see.

To see the dewdrops thrill the blades of grass,
Makes my whole body shake; for here's 'my'
    choice
Of either sun or shade, and both are green –
A Chaffinch laughs in his melodious voice.

The banks are stormed by Speedwell, that 'blue'
    flower
So like a little heaven with one star out;
I see an amber lake of buttercups,
And Hawthorn foams the hedges round about.

The old Oak tree looks now so green and young,
That even swallows perch awhile and sing:
This is that time of year, so sweet and warm,
When bats wait not for stars ere they take wing.

As long as I love Beauty I am young,
Am young or old as I love more or less;
When Beauty is not heeded or seems stale,
My life's a cheat, let Death end my distress.

William Henry Davies

One Spring Day

Dawn-drenched woods beneath a pearl-pale sky,
Gently wakened to the green delight
Of this new day, stretch silken leaves, in shy
Disorder, through the Springtime's lilac air.
Soft scents and sounds brim up from beauty's bowers,
Bright with morning sunlight, fresh with tang
From sheen of glass-cool sea, pearled from shower's
Ling'ring kiss on trembling bloom, and there,
In smiling secrecy, abundance flowers.

When twilight breeze shakes sweetness from the trees,
They tingle with the sunset's vital bronze,
Lighting brilliance in the mind that sees,
Striking hidden tremor in the heart,
While all this burning glory, from the fall
Of one vast evening, flows like fervent prayer –

In silent praise to God, before the call
Of still, delicious night and gift of sleep.

N. Ellis

Life's Nature

You don't have to understand Life's nature,
then it becomes a grand affair.
Let every day just of itself occur
like a child walks away from every hurt
and happens upon the gift of many flowers.

To collect and the blossoms spare,
that never enters the child's mind.
She gently unties them from her hair.
where they were kept captive with such delight.
and the hands of the loving, youthful years
reach out to embrace the new.

Rainer Maria Rilke (tr. Cliff Crego)

The Incoming Of Summer

Where by the stream the towers of the wild hyacinth bore their clustered bells, sought by that gold-vestured hunchback the wild bee, the willow wren sang his little melody, pausing awhile to watch the running water. The early purple orchids grew with the blue-bells, their spurs upraised, their green leaves mottled with purple. Already the blackthorn had put forth its blossoms, a sign of frostless nights and warm days; already the blackbird had planted its nest in the alder bush.... The allotted span of the celandines was over, their rayed spokes of yellow were bleached – the wheatears were flitting upon the swarded downlands. The flowers had gathered to themselves all the light that the sun of early spring had flung between swift clouds, the seeds were formed, their hopes fulfilled. In their place came wild straw-berries and herb robert, the dog-violet and the speedwell.

Henry Williamson

The Meeting-Place

Below there crouched a dream of emerald woods
And gleaming borders solitary as sleep:
Pale waters ran like glimmering threads of pearl.
A sigh was straying among happy leaves;
Cool-perfumed with slow pleasure-burdened feet
Faint stumbling breezes faltered among flowers.
The white crane stood, a vivid motionless streak,
Peacock and parrot jewelled soil and tree,
The dove's soft moan enriched the enamoured air
And fire-winged wild-drakes swam in silvery pools.
At the end reclined a stern and giant tract
Of tangled depths and solemn questioning hills
And peaks like a bare austerity of the soul,
Armoured, remote and desolately grand
Like the thought-screened infinities that lie
Behind the rapt smile of the Almighty's dance.

Aurobindo

Solitude

How still it is here in the woods. The trees
Stand motionless, as if they did not dare
To stir, lest it should break the spell. The air
Hangs quiet as spaces in a marble frieze.
Even this little brook, that runs at ease,
Whispering and gurgling in its knotted bed,
Seems but to deepen, with its curling thread
Of sound, the shadowy sun-pierced silences.
Sometimes a hawk screams or a woodpecker
Startles the stillness from its fixéd mood
With his loud careless tap. Sometimes I hear
The dreamy whitethroat from some far-off tree
Pipe slowly on the listening solitude,
His five pure notes succeeding pensively.

Archibald Lampman

The whole time in the open air, resting at midday, under the
elms with the ripple of heat flowing through the shadow; at
midnight between the ripe corn and the hawthorne hedge on
the white camomile and the poppy pale in the duskiness, with
face upturned to the thoughtful heaven. Consider the glory
of it, the life above this life to be obtained from constant
presence with the sunlight and the stars.

Richard Jefferies

Beech Root

In sparkling sinewy woodland after rain
the ground glitters with diamonds.
On every leaf and blade of grass, drops
of dewy moon, the sun bright encircles.

On the path that canters down
to the sea's white stallions
that inward break
on beach of dark book spines upended,
vermilion fades to peach, a tiny petal
pimpernel like the setting sun
sky stretching;
and another flower nameless
opening in valley grass
shines her pale face twilight
before the violet.

These uncoloured little faces
with heavy rain were washed.

The path to the tumbling sea
clambers a stile, enters an elven wood
whose tips by the sea and salt wind stiff
as heather, are clipped.

Below the path, the stream
in deep brown rocky dell dances,
and each tangle-wood beech at its brink
stands upside down, drinking deep;

for here, the root itself I see upended,
root of a living community
clasping shining fingers, toes in the air;
growing into, flowing out of itself

the labyrinth all exposed for poet,
place for a child to climb and sit,
multiple wild arms mutually embrace,
for the tree you see is in reverse –

the root uplifted, skyward flowers,
branches buried, the earth empowers,
and now the things that are hid, are seen,
and things that are seen, were really
    upside down.

Jane Adams

Rain

In my world of rain and reason
There's a lovely rhythmic sound
That is in the softened silence
As the wet drops hit the ground.

It's a native, earthy music
In a cool responsive note
That soothes the dry, parched hollow
Of the earth's reluctant throat.

It's a sensuous unfolding
In the dampened atmosphere
That's instinctively rewarding
To my music loving ear.

Alison Wyrley Birch

Spring Song

All suddenly, a soft wind blew,
A softened sunlight trembled through,
A warmth shone down on face and hand
And touched with fingers soft the land.

Along the hedge the buds unfold
And in the oaks the starlings scold;

The clouds blow by and leave the sky
A broad blue petal stretched on high.

Peter Adams

– *Optimism* –

These are the soul's changes. I don't believe in ageing.
I believe in forever altering one's aspect to the sun.
Hence my optimism.

Virginia Woolf

Hope is definitely not the same thing as optimism. It is not the conviction that something will turn out well, but the certainty that something makes sense, regardless of how it turns out.

Vaclav Havel

Two men look out through the same bars:
One sees the mud, and one the stars.

Frederick Langbridge

One Life

One SONG can spark a moment
One FLOWER can wake the dream
One TREE can start a forest
One BIRD can herald spring
One SMILE begins a friendship
One HANDSCALSP lifts a soul
One STAR can guide a ship at sea
One WORD can frame the goal
One VOTE can change a nation
One SUNBEAM lights a room
One CANDLE wipes out darkness
One LAUGH will conquer gloom
One STEP must start each journey
One WORD must start a prayer
One HOPE will raise our spirits
One TOUCH can show you care
One VOICE can speak with wisdom
One HEART can know what is true
One LIFE can make a difference.

Anon

The worst is not
So long as we can say 'This is the worst'.

William Shakespeare

I am an optimist, unrepentant and militant. After all, in order not to be a fool an optimist must know how sad a place the world can be. It is only the pessimist who finds this out anew every day.

Peter Ustinov

Life may change, but it may fly not;
Hope may vanish, but can die not;
Truth be veiled, but still it burneth;
Love repulsed, – but it returneth!

Percy Bysshe Shelley

We are all in the gutter,
but some of us are looking at the stars.

Oscar Wilde

Nor greetings where no kindness is, nor all
The dreary intercourse of daily life,
Shall e'er prevail against us, or disturb
Our cheerful faith, that all which we behold
Is full of blessings.

William Wordsworth

It is when we truly know and understand that we have a limited time on earth, and that we have no way of knowing when our time is up, that we will begin to live each day to the fullest, as if it was the only one we had.

Elisabeth Kubler-Ross

An optimist is a man who starts a crossword puzzle
with a fountain pen.

Anon

Optimist – A man who gets treed by a lion
but enjoys the scenery.

Walter Winchell

All is for the best in the best of possible worlds.

Voltaire

'Twixt the optimist and the pessimist
The difference is droll:
The optimist sees the doughnut
But the pessimist sees the hole.

McLandburgh Wilson

The optimist proclaims that we live in the best of all possible worlds; and the pessimist fears this is true.

James Branch Cabell

When the outlook is steeped in pessimism, I remind myself, Two and two still make four, and you can't keep mankind down for long.

Bernard Baruch

An optimist is a person who sees a green light everywhere, while the pessimist sees only the red stop light ... But the truly wise person is color-blind.

Albert Schweitzer

I am an optimist.
It does not seem too much use being anything else.

Sir Winston Churchill

Two knights contended in the list –
An optimist, a pessimist;
But each by mist was blinded so
That neither struck a single blow.

R. T. Wombat

Optimism

Talk happiness. The world is sad enough
Without your woes. No path is wholly rough;
Look for the places that are smooth and clear,
And speak of those, to rest the weary ear
Of Earth, so hurt by one continuous strain
Of human discontent and grief and pain.

Talk faith. The world is better off without
Your uttered ignorance and morbid doubt.
If you have faith in God, or man, or self,
Say so. If not, push back upon the shelf
Of silence all your thoughts, till faith shall come;
No one will grieve because your lips are dumb.

Talk health. The dreary, never-changing tale
Of mortal maladies is worn and stale.
You cannot charm, or interest, or please
By harping on that minor chord, disease.
Say you are well, or all is well with you,
And God shall hear your words and make them true.

Ella Wheeler Wilcox

Optimism is the content of small men in high places.

F. Scott Fitzgerald

– *Philosophy* –

Philosophers sit in their sylvan hall
And talk of the duties of man,
Of Chaos and Cosmos, Hegel and Kant,
With the Oversoul well in the van;
All on their hobbies they amble away
And a terrible dust they make;
Disciples devout both gaze and adore,
As daily they listen and bake.

Louisa M. Alcott

Philosophy is common-sense in a dress suit.

Oliver S. Braston

The philosophy of one century
is the common sense of the next.

Henry Ward Beecher

Metaphysics is the finding of bad reasons
for what we believe on instinct.

Francis Herbert Bradley

Philosophy is the homemade medicine those take
who have not the courage to meet life as it is.

Lucas Cleeve

Old men [reference to Tolstoy] have always been prone to
see the end of the world. The hell with the philosophy of
the great of this world.

Anton Chekhov

You are a philosopher, Dr. Johnson. I have tried, too, in my
time to be a philosopher; but, I don't know how, cheerful-
ness was always breaking in.

Oliver Edwards

One should oblige everyone to the extent of one's ability.
One often needs someone smaller than oneself.

Jean de la Fontaine

The truth is so simple that it is regarded as
pretentious banality.

Dag Hammarskjöld

The Arabians say that Abul Khain, the mystic, and Abu Ali Seena, the philosopher, conferred together; and, on parting, the philosopher said, 'All that he sees I know'; and the mystic said, 'All that he knows I see.'

Ralph Waldo Emerson

The society which scorns excellence in plumbing because plumbing is a humble activity and tolerates shoddiness in philosophy because it is an exalted activity will have neither good plumbing nor good philosophy. Neither its pipes nor its theories will hold water.

John W. Gardner

Society can overlook murder, adultery or swindling; it never forgives the preaching of a new gospel.

Frederick Harrison

A modest confession of ignorance is the ripest and last attainment of philosophy.

Roswell D. Hitchcock

Be a philosopher, but amidst all your philosophy, be still a man.

David Hume

A bilious philosopher's opinion of the world can only be accepted with a pinch of salt, of Epsom salt by preference.

Aldous Huxley

Metaphysics may be, after all, only the art of being sure of something that is not so, and logic only the art of going wrong with confidence.

Joseph Wood Krutch

Be quiet and people will think you are a philosopher.

Old Latin Proverb

Yet the deepest truths are best read between the lines, and, for the most part, refuse to be written.

Amos Bronson Alcott

A truth that's told with bad intent
Beats all the lies you can invent.

William Blake

Truth has a way of shifting under pressure.

Curtis Bok

Facts that are not frankly faced
have a habit of stabbing us in the back.

Sir Harold Bowden

For truth there is no deadline.

Heywood Broun

Can there be a more horrible object in existence
than an eloquent man not speaking the truth?

Thomas Carlyle

They decided that all liars should be whipped.
And a man came along and told them the truth.
And they hanged him.

T. W. H. Crosland

Truth is such a rare thing, it is delightful to tell it.

Emily Dickinson

The truth doesn't hurt unless it ought to.

B. C. Forbes

Craft must have clothes, but truth loves to go naked.

Thomas Fuller

Truth always lags behind, limping along
on the arm of time.

Baltasar Gracian

Back From the Shopping

I do not bring you answers,
for no man can give
the answers that another man
must find to live

The questions that would
drag me to the floor
have slipped out through the holes
to leave my bag so light
that nothing's in it any more.

So if you search for light,
just flip the switch,
or stick your head
outside the door.

Kevan Myers

– *Prudence* –

The wise man knows that the very polestar of prudence
lies in steering by the wind.

Baltasar Gracián

Prudence is a lovely quality. This teaches us to speak every word, and perform every action of life, at a proper time, in the proper place, and toward the proper person. It is prudence that distinguishes our various behaviour toward our fellow creatures, according to their different ranks and degrees among mankind, or the different relations in which we stand to them. It is a very desirable excellency to know when it is proper to speak, and when it is best to keep silence; at what seasons, and in what company, we should awaken our zeal, and exert our active powers; or when we should hide ourselves, or put a bridle upon our lips, and sit still, and hear.

Without a prudent determination in matters before us, we shall be plunged into perpetual errors.

Dr I. Watts

The one prudence in life is concentration;
the one evil is dissipation.

Ralph Waldo Emerson

There is always much to be said for not attempting more than you can do, and for making a certainty of what you try. But this principle, like others in life, has its exceptions.

Sir Winston Churchill

Vices enter into the composition of virtues as poisons into the composition of certain medicines. Prudence and common sense mix them together, and make excellent use of them against the misfortunes that attend human life.

Duc de la Rochefoucauld

Truth, but not the whole truth, must be the invariable principle of every man who hath either religion, honour, or prudence. Those who violate it, may be cunning, but they are not able. Lies and perfidy are the refuge of fools and cowards.

Philip Dormer Stanhope

Do you come to a philosopher as to a cunning man, to learn something by magic or witchcraft, beyond what can be known by common prudence and discretion?

David Hume

The one prudence in life is concentration; the one evil is dissipation: and it makes no difference whether our dissipations are coarse or fine; property and its cares, friends and a social habit, or politics, or music, or feasting. Everything is good which takes away one plaything and delusion more, and drives us home to add one stroke of faithful work.

Ralph Waldo Emerson

Economy, prudence, and a simple life are the sure masters of need, and will often accomplish that which their opposites, with a fortune at hand, will fail to do.

Clara Barton

Men do not fail commonly for want of knowledge, but for want of prudence to give wisdom the preference.

The merchants and company have long laughed at transcendentalism, higher laws, etc., crying, 'None of your moonshine', as if they were anchored to something not only definite, but sure and permanent. If there was any institution which was presumed to rest on a solid and secure basis, and more than any other represented this boasted common sense, prudence, and practical talent, it was the bank; and now those very banks are found to be mere reeds shaken by the wind. Scarcely one in the land has kept its promise.

Henry David Thoreau

Prudence

Seek not the things that others seek;
Say not the words that others speak;
Do not the works that others do;
Just do the ones that well suit you.

Live not the ways that others live;
Give not the things that others give;
Learn not the ways that others learn;
Earn not the ways that others earn.

Think not the ways that others think;
Ink not the way that others ink;
Sing not the way that others sing;
Do just things that contentment bring.

Take just the things in others good;
Eat just the needed healthy food;
Copy what is exemplary;
Just take what you can well carry!

Dr John Celes

Want of prudence is too frequently the want of virtue

Oliver Goldsmith

Prudence

Mortal Prudence, handmaid of divine Providence, hath inscrutable reckoning with Fate and Fortune: We sail a changeful sea through halcyon days and storm, and when the ship laboureth, our stedfast purpose trembles like as the compass in a binnacle. Our stability is but balance, and conduct lies in masterful administration of the unforseen.

Robert Bridges From *The Testament of Beauty*

Prudence is the necessary ingredient in all the virtues, without which they degenerate into folly and excess

Jeremy Collier

The great must submit to the dominion of prudence and of virtue, or none will long submit to the dominion of the great.

Edmund Burke

The rich endowments of the mind are temperance, prudence, and fortitude. Prudence is a universal virtue, which enters into the composition of all the rest; and where she is not, fortitude loses its name and nature.

Voltaire

Prudence is a conformity to the rules of reason, truth, and decency, at all times and in all circumstances.

Let prudence always attend your pleasures; it is the way to enjoy the sweets of them, and not be afraid of the consequences.

Anon

The bounds of a man's knowledge are easily concealed
if he has but prudence

OliverGoldsmith

A bird in the hand is worth two in the bush.

Proverb

Forewarned is forearmed.

Proverb

For want of a nail the shoe was lost;
for want of a shoe the horse was lost;
for want of a horse the rider was lost.

Proverb

Prevention is better than cure.

Proverb

The Value of Planning

The best way to make the most of your life is to take the long look ahead. The immediate situation may seem confused and unpromising. That means all the more opportunity for intelligence; for planning; for foundations laid on the bedrock of worth and virtue; for patient building; and for courageous pioneering. Be not afraid. You are greater than the things about you. You stand on a pinnacle of possibility, and the future will be largely what you make it. Begin where you are. Act, and above all, plan. This booklet will tell you how to begin planning. Let no one tell you that life is too uncertain to plan. Every great victory of the human race has been won in spite of the cry that it could not be done. You can plan and lose and plan again, rising higher each time because of the purpose and discipline of your life. Learn to plan by planning.

Anon

It is always good
When a man has two irons in the fire.

Francis Beaumont

Put your trust in God, my boys,
and keep your powder dry.

Valentine Blacker

The Camel

Study the camel, who has learned to wait
Impassive under load piled upon load,
Then kicked, told to un-kneel, and tread
    no-road
Out of the blessed shade of palm and date
Across the desert and the herbless state
Where nothing may be reaped, and nothing
    sowed,
His only nourishment the prodding goad,
Beneath the sun's intensity of hate.

But he is obstinate, he foots the sand
Slowly, rhythmically, day by day,
Ignoring admonition and the rod.
Wisdom we humans cannot understand
Curves his ironic lip. In his own way
He knows the hidden hundredth name for God.

Richard Church

I'd much rather have that fellow
    inside my tent pissing out,
than outside my tent pissing in.

Lyndon B. Johnson

Any girl who was a lady would not even think of having
such a good time that she did not remember to hang on to
her jewelry.

Anita Loos

Be nice to people on your way up
because you'll meet 'em on your way down.

Wilson Mizner

– *Rapture* –

My Joy Is So Quiet

My joy is so quiet,

I could easily pass it by.

Only my attentive soul is aware of it,

As it beckons in the sunlight that falls through
the doorway

Or shines in rays refreshed by the storm,

Elusive my joy and fleet,

Shimmering as the rainbow arch

'Twixt sun and shower,

Yet strong to uphold.

Softly I cross with feathered tread
This airy bridge, this bow of light
To the gold of the life beyond.

Eleanor Trives

Rapture

Overwhelmed his limbs and round his soul became
A fiery ocean of felicity:
He foundered drowned in sweet and burning vasts:
The dire delight that could shatter mortal flesh,
The rapture that the gods sustain he bore.
Immortal pleasure cleansed him in its waves
And turned his strength into undying power.
Immortality captured Time and carried Life.
Trembling with the beauty of a wordless speech,
And thoughts too great and deep to find a voice,
Thoughts whose desire new-makes the universe.
A scale of sense that climbed with fiery feet
To heights of unimagined happiness,
Recast his being's aura in joy-glow,
His body glimmered like a skyey shell;
His gates to the world were swept with seas of light.
His earth, dowered with celestial competence,
Harboured a power that needed now no more
To cross the closed customs-line of mind and flesh

SERENDIPITY

And smuggle godhead into humanity …
In sudden moments of revealing flame,
In passionate responses half-unveiled
He reached the rim of ecstasies unknown;
A touch supreme surprised his hurrying heart,
The clasp was remembered of the wonderful,
And hints leaped down of white beatitudes.
Eternity drew close disguised as Love
And laid its hand upon the body of Time.
A little gift comes from the Immensitudes,
But measureless to life its gain of joy;
All the untold Beyond is mirrored there.
A giant drop of the Bliss unknowable.

Aurobindo

– *Serendipity* –

Anything Can Happen

Listen to the Mustn'ts, child,
Listen to the Don'ts
Listen to the Shouldn'ts
The Impossibles, the Won'ts
Listen to the Never Haves,

211

Then listen close to me –
Anything can happen, child,
Anything can be.

Shel Silverstein

Bright Intervals

When we have planned an outing and we want the sun
    to shine
we listen to the forecast, hoping that it will be fine
and oh, the disappointment when we hear the
    prophets say,
'Showery, with bright intervals'
that means a rainy day!...
Life is like the weather, with bright intervals and
    showers
Days of smiles
 and days of tears
then unexpected hours
of peace and satisfaction in the midst of dire distress
Storm and trouble followed by a quiet happiness ...
This is Life; calamity
then joy to compensate
if we had a cloudless sky should we appreciate
the meaning of real happiness?
Thus does the spirit grow
and overcome its failures and the griefs of human woe ...

So when you are sad at heart, defeated and subdued

God sends you His bright intervals

and then with hope renewed

you can go on, discerning through the dark the sun's
    bright beams

bright intervals of faith reborn and high undaunted
    dreams.

Patience Strong

– *Strength* –

Inspiration

Go on; go on; go on;

Strive from morning to the next dawn.

Make your convictions felt.

Someday all wars will be quelled.

Go forth; go forth; go forth.

Spread peace throughout the earth.

Leave your mark for all to see.

Greed and devastation are no longer a need.

Be strong; be strong; be strong;

No right was gotten by a wrong.

Let no one distract you from your goal.

Your ideas must be told.

Have faith; have faith; have faith.

We must save the human race.

All nation, in cooperation join hands.

Let friendship be our stand.

Look up; look up; look up.

Our guidance comes from above.

No bombs or missiles should we see.

Tis glorious when peace is a reality.

J. P. Kennedy

Life begets life. Energy creates energy. It is by spending
oneself that one becomes rich.

Sarah Bernhardt

The using up of strength is in a certain sense still an increase
of strength; for fundamentally it is only a matter of a wide
circle: all the strength we give away comes back over us
again, experienced and transformed.

Rainer Maria Rilke

There are certain days when one seems to have the strength
of some gigantic and prehistoric monster. It has been so
with me today ...

All day my mind has reached out and out. I have thought of everyone and everything. Minute little happenings in the lives of many people have been revealed to me. Today, had I a dozen hands, I could write a dozen tales, strange wonderful tales, all at one time.

Sherwood Anderson

There are few of us who have not a strong propensity to diminish our present strength by entertaining fears of future weakness.

Charles B. Fairbanks

It is not good to see people who have been pretending strength all their lives lose it even for a minute.

Lillian Hellman

The greater the contrast, the greater is the potential. Great energy only comes from a correspondingly great tension between opposites.

C. G. Jung

I felt invincible. My strength was that of a giant. God was certainly standing by me. I smashed five saloons with rocks before I ever took a hatchet.

Carry Nation

It is the devil to be struggling forward, like a man in the mire, and making not an inch by your exertions, and such seems to be my fate.

Sir Walter Scott

Everything is bound to take up room and to shove other things aside in some measure: the question is to understand justly what hold each thing has normally in nature and in human nature, and how great is the ascension or flowering of life that it is capable of producing.

George Santayana

Sweat and effort, human nature strained to its uttermost and on the rack, yet getting through alive, and then turning its back on its success to pursue another more rare and arduous still – this is the sort of thing the presence of which inspires us.

William James

We deceive ourselves when we fancy that
only weakness needs support. Strength needs it far more.

Madame Swetchine

One day in retrospect the years of struggle
will strike you as the most beautiful.

Sigmund Freud

Why Worry?

40% will never happen, for anxiety is the result of a
tired mind,

30% concerns old decisions which cannot be altered,

12% centers in criticisms, mostly untrue, made by people
who feel inferior,

10% is related to my health which worsens while I worry,

and only 8% is 'legitimate', showing that life does have real
problems which may be met head-on when I have
eliminated senseless worries.

Anon

Spiritual Exercise

Every trouble is an opportunity to win the grace of strength.
Whatever else trouble is in the world for, it is here for this
good purpose – to develop strength. For a trouble is a moral
and spiritual task. It is something which is hard to do. And
it is in the spiritual world as in the physical, strength is
increased by encounter with the difficult. A world without
any trouble in it would be, to people of our kind, a place of

spiritual enervation and moral laziness. Fortunately, every day is crowded with care. Every day to every one of us brings its questions, its worries, and its tasks, brings its sufficiency of trouble. Thus we get our daily spiritual exercise. Every day we are blessed with new opportunities for the development of strength of soul.

George Hodges

You are assertive

If you can say no without being aggressive, and can stand up for yourself without offending anyone, you can be confident of remaining in control of any situation.

For every problem there is a solution

Adopt this attitude and you will be confident that you can cope with everything.

He that wrestles with us strengthens our nerves and sharpens our skill. Our antagonist is our helper.

Edmund Burke

Hell is full of the talented but Heaven of the energetic.

St Jane Frances de Chantal

Battering Through Living

Bows break into the dark,
broach inch by inch the towering water welter.
The shock of each gained impact
fuses in brilliance that illuminates
a flash, the long and heaving plain.
Then dark, and the upward battering
on, relentless into the dark.
Bone strakes and timber muscles ache
and groan. Glance back, and for a
spell delight in easier seas foreknown.
But these no longer hold a rapture.
Once passed and dropped, such soundings
ring a hollow and a wrecking clang.

See, with passage through unplumbed waters,
our stem still furrows the dark,
though we rest.
Even because of the waters' strength
we gather
and twist with purpose, and
bows bite into the dark.

Peter Adams

Be Strong!

BE STRONG!
We are not here to play, to dream, to drift;
We have hard work to do and loads to lift;
Shun not the struggle – face it; 'tis God's gift.

BE STRONG!
Say not, 'The days are evil. Who's to blame?'
And fold the hands and acquiesce – oh, shame!
Stand up, speak out, and bravely, in God's name.

BE STRONG!
It matters not how deep intrenched the wrong,
How hard the battle goes, the day how long;
Faint not – fight on! Tomorrow comes the song.

Maltbie Davenport Babcock

If

If you think you are beaten, you are.
If you think you dare not, you don't.
If you'd like to win, but think you can't,
It's almost certain you won't
If you think you'll lose, you've lost.
For out of the world we find
Success begins with a fellow's will.

It's all in the state of mind.
If you think you're outclassed, you are.
You've got to think high to rise.
You've got to be sure of yourself before
You can ever win a prize.
Life's battles don't always go
To the stronger or faster person.
But sooner or later the person who wins
Is the one who thinks they can.

Anon

– *Success* –

Built Together

There are parts of a ship which taken by themselves would sink. The engine would sink. The propeller would sink. But when the parts of a ship are built together, they float. So with the events of my life. Some have been tragic. Some have been happy. But when they are built together, they form a craft that floats and is going someplace. And I am comforted.

Ralph W. Sockman

Road To Success

Throw away all ambition beyond that of doing the day's work well. The travelers on the road to success live in the present, heedless of taking thought for the morrow. Live neither in the past nor in the future, but let each day's work absorb your entire energies, and satisfy your widest ambition.

William Osler

Management is efficiency in climbing the ladder of success; leadership determines whether the ladder is standing against the right wall.

Stephen R. Covey,
from *The Seven Habits of Highly Effective People*

Success

Before God's footstool to confess
The poor soul knelt and bowed his head.
'I failed,' he wailed. The Master said,
'Thou didst thy best – that is success.'

Anon

The key to success isn't much good
until one discovers the right lock to insert it in.

Tehyi Hsieh

The Secret

Whenever you see a successful business,
someone once made a courageous decision.

Peter Drucker

Never Give Up

When you get into a tight place and everything goes against
you, till it seems as though you could not hang on a minute
longer, never give up then, for that is just the place and time
that the tide will turn.

Harriet Beecher Stowe

Success

Success is to be measured
not so much by the position that one has reached in life
as by the obstacles which he has overcome
while trying to succeed.

Booker T. Washington

Success, which is something so simple in the end,
is made up of thousands of things, we never fully know
what they are.

Rainer Maria Rilke

'Twixt failure and success the point's so fine
Men sometimes know not when they touch the line.
Just when the pearl was waiting one more plunge,
How many a struggler has thrown up the sponge! ...
Then take this honey from the bitterest cup:
'There is no failure save in giving up!'

Henry Austin

There is only one success – to be able to spend your life
in your own way.

Christopher Morley

If a man be self-controlled, truthful, wise, and resolute, is
there aught that can stay out of the reach of such a man?

***Panchatantra*, 3**

There is no success without hardship.

Sophocles, *Electra*

If at first you do succeed,
don't take any more chances.

Kin Hubbard

Circumstances

'People are always blaming their circumstances for what they are,' Vivie exclaims in contempt and disgust. 'I don't believe in circumstances. The people who get on in this world are the people who get up and look for the circumstances they want, and, if they can't find them, make them.' She may be forgiven much for that valiant remark.

St John Ervine

Social Success

The pursuit of social success, in the form of prestige or power or both, is the most important obstacle to happiness in a competitive society. I am not denying that success is an ingredient in happiness – to some, a very important ingredient. But it does not, by itself, suffice to satisfy most people. You may be rich and admired, but if you have no friends, no interests, no spontaneous useless pleasures, you will be miserable. Living for social success is one form of living by a theory, and all living by theory is dusty and desiccating.

Bertrand Russell

– *Wisdom* –

When Wisdom tells me that the world's a speck
Lost on the shoreless blue of God's To-Day …
I smile, and think, 'For every man his way:
The world's my ship, and I'm alone on deck!'
And when he tells me that the world's a spark
Lit in the whistling gloom of God's To-Night …
I look within me to the edge of dark,
And dream, 'The world's my field, and I'm the lark,
Alone with upward song, alone with light!'

Siegfried Sassoon

Acting

It is easier to get an actor to be a cowboy
than to get a cowboy to be an actor.

John Ford

Wisdom

O world, thou choosest not the better part!
It is not wisdom to be only wise,
And on the inward vision close the eyes;
But it is wisdom to believe the heart.
Columbus found a world, and had no chart

Save one that faith deciphered in the skies;
To trust the soul's invincible surmise
Was all his science and his only art.
Our knowledge is a torch of smoky pine
That lights the pathway but one step ahead
Across a void of mystery and dread.
Bid, then, the tender light of faith to shine
By which alone the mortal heart is led
Unto the thinking of the thought divine.

George Santayana

Capacity To Believe

This capacity to believe is the most significant and fundamental human faculty, and the most important thing about a man is what he believes in the depth of his being. This is the thing that makes him what he is; the thing that organizes him and feeds him; the thing that keeps him going in the face of untoward circumstances; the thing that gives him resistance and drive. Let neutrality, confusion, indifference, or skepticism enter this inner place, and the very springs of life will cease to flow.

Hugh Stevenson Tigner

Time is the most valuable thing a man can spend.

Theophrastus

Diligence is the mother of good luck,
and God gives all things to industry.

Benjamin Franklin

You will never know what is enough
unless you know what is more than enough.

William Blake

Aspire to greatness.
Each of us is going to travel the road of life's adventure
only once, but once is enough if you do it right.

J. Warren McClure

My philosophy is that only you are responsible for your life,
but doing the best at this moment puts you in the best place
for the next moment.

Oprah Winfrey

The heights by great men reached and kept
Were not attained by sudden flight,
But they, while their companions slept,
Were toiling upward in the night.

Henry Wadsworth Longfellow

Heart-throbs

Knowledge is happiness, because to have knowledge – broad
deep knowledge – is to know true ends from false, and lofty
things from low. To know the thoughts and deeds that have
marked man's progress is to feel the great heart-throbs of
humanity through the centuries; and if one does not feel in
these pulsations a heavenward striving, one must indeed be
deaf to the harmonies of life.

Helen Keller

The journey of a thousand miles begins with one step.

Lao-Tse

To be a philosopher is not merely to have subtle thoughts,
nor even to found a school, but so to love wisdom as to live,
according to its dictates, a life of simplicity, independence,
magnanimity, and trust.

Henry David Thoreau

Knowledge is proud that it knows so much;
wisdom is humble that it knows no more.

William Cowper

Besides the noble art of getting things done, there is the noble art of leaving things undone. The wisdom of life consists in the elimination of nonessentials.

Lin Yutang

Guiding Ideals

Merely to study problems is not enough. It is also necessary to search fearlessly for truth, to reach one's own conclusions, and to beware of indoctrinators and propagandists. Above all we need to remember that the difference between training and education is the difference between studying with narrow aims and studying with broad ones. Economic problems need to be studied with the aim not only of getting America out of debt, for example, but mainly of making possible the abundant life for all citizens. Psychological problems should be studied with the aim not only of curing particular ailments, but of growing harmoniously in all aspects of living. The most humanitarian, balanced, enduring aims possible are the most important key to sound conclusions and clear thinking. Superficial things change; ideals abide.

Anon

It takes a wise man to recognize a wise man.

Xenophanes

I find the great thing in this world is not so much where
we stand as in what direction we are moving.

Oliver Wendell Holmes

Nothing is so exhausting as indecision,
and nothing is so futile.

Bertrand Russell

Both in the Same Boat

As the professor of literature was getting into the boat he
said to the boatman: 'Tell me, my good man, have you ever
studied grammar?'

'No, sir,' the boatman replied.

'Alas,' said the professor loftily, 'what a pity. Without such
knowledge you've wasted half your life'.

The boat set off. Not long after, a storm blew up. The boat
was caught in a whirlpool.

The boatman shouted above the chaos: 'Tell me, sir, have
you ever learned to swim?'

'No, no!' the professor cried.

'Alas', the boatman replied, 'what a pity. Without such
knowledge you've wasted all your life!'

Idries Shah

– *Wonder* –

Let others wrangle, I will wonder.

John Lubbock

The world will never starve for want of wonders;
but only for want of wonder.

G. K. Chesterton

Wonder

I kiss my hand
To the stars, lovely asunder
Starlight, wafting him out of it; and
Glow, glory in thunder …
Since though he is under the world's
Splendour and wonder,
His mystery must be instressed, stressed;
For I greet him the days I meet him,
And bless when I understand

Gerald Manley Hopkins
From 'The Wreck of the Deutschland'

Wonder … is essentially an 'opening' attitude – an awareness that there is more to life than one has yet fathomed, an experience of new vistas in life to be explored as well as new profundities to be plumbed.

Rollo May

Wonder is the qualitative distance which God placed between man and truth. It enables man to find the truth.

Theodor Haecker

Wonder Is Not Precisely Knowing

Wonder is not precisely knowing,
And not precisely knowing not,
A beautiful but bleak condition
He has not lived who has not felt.

Suspense is his maturer sister;
Whether adult delight is pain
Or of itself a new misgiving –
This is the gnat that mangles men.

Emily Dickenson

The 'Ah' Of Wonder

The 'Ah' of wonder
Attempting a definition,

A brief intense forgetting of self.
A leaf away from the 'me',
When the rose
Unfolds,

When the stars
Arise,

And the eyes
Widen with love
For everything that is.

A. Sammaan-Hanna

Time

Life's a gamble
Life's a scramble
Fret and turmoil
strife and noise;
Life's a worry
what's the hurry?
Give me peace and quiet joys.

Life's all clamour
fake and glamour
tinsel shams and vulgar show
Fight for money
aren't folks funny?
rushing madly to and fro.
Give me leisure
simple pleasure
time in which to stand and stare;
time to wonder
time to wander
time to dream, and time to spare …
Time for gazing
time for raising
weary eyes to leaf and wing
time for praying
time for saying
Thank You God for everything.

Patience Strong

Let others wrangle, I will wonder.

St Augustine

From Midnight

I have thrown wide my window
    And looked upon the night,
And seen Arcturus burning
    In chaos, proudly bright.

The powdered stars above me
    Have littered heaven's floor –
A thousand I remember;
    I saw a myriad more.

I have forgotten thousands
    For deep and deep between,
My mind built up the darkness
    Of space, unheard, unseen.

I held my hands to heaven
    To hold perfection there,
But through my fingers streaming
    Went time, as thin as air;

Michael Roberts

Secrets

Secrets lie in human hearts

the secrets of the years

Little secret vanities, and little secret fears

Memories of bygone things too precious to be told

Treasured in the quiet heart till we are tired and old ...

Things unspoken

hidden hopes

and dreams we dare not tell

Like bright jewels dropped into the depths of some
    'dark' well

So beware of open ears, of tongues and prying eyes

We should keep our secrets locked away if we
    were wise ...

God Who made this lovely world

He has His secrets too

Man cannot find the secret of the wonders He can do

Though we fall upon our knees and ask with
    every breath

God keeps the secrets of creation, and of life and death.

Patience Strong

– *Work* –

My wife's idea of housecleaning
is to sweep the room at a glance.

Joey Adams

The shorter the hours, the larger the income. Don't get into
the habit of putting in long hours or you may be set down
into a permanent subordinate position.

George Ade

We have it on good authority that it is lawful to pull an ass
out of the pit on the Sabbath day. Well, there never was a
bigger ass, nor a deeper pit.

Henry Ward Beecher

It's better to be in love with your work
than in love with your self.

The best grease is elbow-grease.
Work now, or wince later.
Sinecures are never long secure.

B. C. Forbes

Anyone can do any amount of work provided it isn't the work he is supposed to be doing at that moment.

I do most of my work sitting down; that's where I shine.

Robert Benchley

Never work before breakfast; if you have to work before breakfast, get your breakfast first.

Josh Billings

A wife is afraid of having her husband enjoy his work too much; she doesn't mind if he suffers at it – for her sake.

Hal Boyle

It is better to wear out than to rust out.

Richard Cumberland, Bishop of Peterborough

All work and no play makes Jack a dull boy,
All play and no work makes Jack a mere toy.

Maria Edgeworth

A Song of Triumph

WORK!
Thank God for the might of it,
The ardour, the urge, the delight of it –
Work that springs from the heart's desire,
Setting the brain and the soul on fire –
Oh, what is so good as the heat of it,
And what is so glad as the beat of it,
And what is so kind as the stern command,
Challenging brain and heart and hand?

WORK!
Thank God for the pride of it,
For the beautiful, conquering tide of it,
Sweeping the life in its furious flood,
Thrilling the arteries, cleansing the blood,
Mastering the stupor and dull despair,
Moving the dreamer to do and dare.
Oh, what is so good as the urge of it,
And what is so glad as the surge of it,
And what is so strong as the summons deep,
Rousing the torpid soul from sleep?

WORK!
Thank God for the pace of it,
For the terrible, keen, swift race of it;

Fiery steeds in full control,
Nostrils a-quiver to greet the goal.
Work, the Power that drives behind,
Guiding the purposes, taming the mind,
Holding the runaway wishes back,
Reining the will to one steady track,
Speeding the energies faster, faster,
Triumphing over disaster.
Oh, what is so good as the pain of it,
And what is so great as the gain of it?
And what is so kind as the cruel goad,
Forcing us on through the rugged road?

WORK!
Thank God for the swing of it,
For the clamouring, hammering ring of it,
Passion and labour daily hurled
On the mighty anvils of the world.
Oh, what is so fierce as the flame of it
And what is so huge as the aim of it?
Thundering on through dearth and doubt,
Calling the plan of the Maker out.
Work, the Titan; Work, the friend,
Shaping the earth to a glorious end,
Draining the swamps and blasting the hills,
Doing whatever the Spirit wills –

Rending a continent apart,
To answer the dream of the Master hears.
Thank God for a world where none may shirk –
Thank God for the Splendour of work!

Angela Morgan

His sole concern with work
was considering how he might best avoid it.

Anatole France

Why work at Nothing, like the Wee Pig's Tail
That Wiggles all day long to no avail?

Irish Proverb

Work is the greatest thing in the world,
so we should always save some of it for tomorrow.

Don Herold

Th' feller who quits work in th' evenin' like he wuz leavin'
a penitentiary never reaches Easy Street.

Frank McKinney

I like work; it fascinates me. I can sit and look at it for hours. I love to keep it by me: the idea of getting rid of it nearly breaks my heart.

Jerome K. Jerome

– *Worry* –

If the grass is greener in the other fellow's yard –
let him worry about cutting it.

Fred Allen

Nobody should ever look anxious
except those who have no anxiety.

Benjamin Disraeli

As a cure for worrying, work is better than whiskey.

Thomas A. Edison

The reason worry kills more people than work
is that more people worry than work.

Robert Frost

It's wonderful what a run there is on worry
when you consider that it never helped anything.

Frank McKinney

Worry, the interest paid by those who borrow trouble.

George W. Lyon

Worry makes everybody thin except fat people
who worry over their fatness.

Reflections of a Bachelor (anon.)

Care to our coffin adds a nail, no doubt,
And every grin so merry draws one out.

John Wolcot

Index by Author